AI for **Therapists**

The Practical Guide to HIPAA-Compliant AI Tools, Prompt Engineering, and Ethical Workflows for Mental Health Professionals

Arrow Jay Publishing
Fort Pierce, Florida | 2026

A Note on AI-Assisted Writing:
This book was researched, structured, and written with the assistance of AI tools. All content has been reviewed, edited, and approved by the publisher. The use of AI in the preparation of this manuscript is consistent with the principles described throughout this book, that AI is a productivity tool that amplifies human judgment, not a replacement for it.

AI for Therapists is part of the AI for Professionals Series.

ISBN (Paperback): 978-1-964326-03-0

ISBN (eBook): 978-1-964326-04-7

First Edition, 2026

Introduction

Dr. Maya Chen, a licensed clinical psychologist in private practice in Miami, used to dread Sunday evenings. After a week of 25 back-to-back sessions, she'd sit at her kitchen table until midnight, staring at a backlog of progress notes, treatment plan updates, and resource handouts that needed drafting. The paperwork never ended. Her caseload felt manageable in theory, but the administrative weight (charting every nuance, every intervention, every client insight) left her exhausted before Monday morning even arrived. She loved the work: the quiet breakthroughs, the moments of genuine connection, the privilege of walking alongside people through their darkest hours. But the endless documentation was stealing that joy. She felt herself slipping into the burnout she so often helped her clients escape.

One evening in early 2026, after yet another late night, Maya read about HIPAA-compliant AI tools designed specifically for behavioral health. Skeptical but desperate for relief, she signed up for a trial of a specialized platform. She started small: anonymized session summaries fed into carefully crafted prompts that generated draft DAP notes in minutes instead of hours. She reviewed, edited, and signed off, always with full human oversight. Within weeks, she reclaimed 8-10 hours per week. Those reclaimed hours became space for deeper reflection, better self-care, and even a few extra clients who needed her. For the first time in years, Maya felt present again, not just surviving her practice, but thriving in it.

Maya's story is no longer exceptional. In March 2026, mental health professionals across the country are quietly transforming their practices with ethical, compliant AI integration. The shift is driven by necessity: unprecedented demand for services collides with persistent administrative burdens and clinician burnout.

According to the American Psychological Association's 2025 Practitioner Pulse Survey (released December 2025, with trends continuing into 2026), 56% of psychologists reported using AI tools to assist with their work at least once in the past year, nearly double the 29% from 2024. Monthly use jumped to 29% (from 11% the prior year), and 8% now use AI daily. The most common applications? Administrative relief: drafting emails and materials (52%), generating content (33%), summarizing notes or articles (32%), and note-taking (22%). Direct clinical uses remain rare (only 8% for diagnosis assistance and 5% for client-facing chatbots) reflecting the field's cautious, ethics-first approach.

Burnout statistics underscore why this matters. Therapists report the highest rates of mental fatigue among healthcare specialties, with 77% experiencing significant exhaustion (Tebra 2025 Physician Burnout Survey). Documentation alone consumes approximately 35% of working hours, over eight hours per week in a typical 30-client schedule (Eleos Health and Reframe Practice data, 2026). Tebra's survey identifies charting as the top burnout driver (tied with low compensation at 23%), fueling a cycle where administrative overload erodes the very empathy and presence that define effective therapy.

Meanwhile, the broader AI-in-behavioral-health market reflects explosive growth: valued at around $55-59 billion in 2025, projections show it reaching $115-124 billion by 2034-2035 (CAGR 7.65-7.69%, per Towards Healthcare and MetaTech Insights). Specialized tools, note generators, progress trackers, and resource creators, are maturing rapidly, offering real efficiency without compromising care.

Yet opportunity comes with responsibility. The APA's Ethical Guidance for AI in the Professional Practice of Health Service Psychology (June 2025, updated December 2025) is clear: AI must augment, never replace, human judgment. Psychologists retain full accountability. Key imperatives include transparency with clients, rigorous bias mitigation, data privacy safeguards (HIPAA compliance mandatory), and unwavering human oversight. Concerns remain high, 92% of psychologists express worries about risks like breaches, bias, and inaccurate outputs (2025 Pulse Survey) and rightly so. The field refuses to sacrifice the irreplaceable human elements of therapy for convenience.

This book is your roadmap through that tension. Written for licensed mental health professionals, psychologists, counselors, clinical social workers, marriage and family therapists in private practice, clinics, or agencies, it offers a practical, ethics-first guide to integrating AI safely and effectively.

What you'll find here:

- Foundations (Chapters 1-3): The 2026 landscape, ethical principles (APA/ACA), and HIPAA essentials.
- Skills (Chapters 4-6): Prompt engineering mastery, from basics to therapist-specific safety nets, plus a ready-to-use prompt library.
- Workflows (Chapters 7-10): Step-by-step applications for session prep, documentation, in-between-session support, and

client-facing resources, all with strict boundaries.

- Implementation & Beyond (Chapters 11-15): Tool comparisons, rollout plans, case studies, burnout prevention, and future trends.

This is not a replacement for professional judgment, legal advice, or clinical training. It provides educational guidance only. Always consult your licensing board, malpractice carrier, HIPAA expert, and ethics resources before adopting any tool or workflow.

If you're a therapist feeling buried under notes, questioning your sustainability, or simply curious about how AI might serve your practice without compromising its heart, this book is for you! Turn the page. Let's reclaim the time and energy you deserve, so you can bring your full presence to the people who need it most.

Quick Start: Your First 30 Minutes with AI

This section is for the therapist who wants results today. Skip the theory for now , you can read the full book at your own pace. Right now, follow these three steps and you will have a working AI documentation workflow before your next session.

What you need before you start: A free trial account with either Twofold Health (twofold.health) or Mentalyc (mentalyc.com). Both offer free trials. Sign the BAA during signup (it takes 60 seconds and is non-negotiable) before entering any client-adjacent information. We are not using commercially available platforms like ChatGPT, Claude and Gemini until you understand what you can and cannot do with them.

Step 1 - Try One Note (10 minutes)

After your next session, spend 3 minutes writing anonymized bullet points of what happened. No client name, no dates, no identifying details. Just: what the client discussed, what intervention you used, how they responded, what you are planning next.

Paste those bullets into your tool with this prompt:

Read the output. Edit what needs editing. You just saved 30 minutes.

Step 2 - Try One Session Prep (10 minutes)

Before your next appointment, paste an anonymized summary of the client's recent progress into the tool with this prompt:

Use it as a starting point, not a script. Edit it to match your voice and your knowledge of the client.

Step 3 - Save Your Prompts (10 minutes)

Open a document and name it My Prompt Library. Paste in both prompts above. Every time you refine a prompt and it works well, save it here with a brief note about when to use it. This library will become one of the most valuable professional tools in your practice.

That is it. You have started. The rest of this book will deepen your skills, expand your toolkit, and help you integrate AI safely across every area of your practice. But the most important step was the one you just took.

Now read Chapter 1 and build on this foundation.

Contents

1. Introduction to AI in Mental Health Practice 1
2. The Ethical Landscape: Guidelines, Risks, and Responsibilities 7
3. HIPAA, Privacy, and Data Security for AI Use 13
4. Prompt Engineering Basics - From Beginner to Advanced 19
5. Building Safe, Effective Prompts - Core Principles for Therapists 26
6. Working With the Prompt Library - A Category-by-Category Workflow Guide 34
7. AI-Assisted Session Preparation and Planning 50
8. Documentation, Progress Notes, and Treatment Planning with AI 58
9. In-Session and Between-Session Support - Ethical Applications 66
10. Client-Facing Tools - Handouts, Resources, and Homework (with Boundaries) 73
11. Comparing AI Tools for Therapists in 2026 - General vs. Specialized 80

12. Step-by-Step Implementation - From First Use to Full Integration 87

13. Case Studies - Real-World Wins, Pitfalls, and Lessons Learned 94

14. Burnout Reduction, Self-Care, and Long-Term Sustainability 101

15. The Future of AI in Psychotherapy - Trends, Predictions, and Staying Ahead 107

Appendix A: Comprehensive Prompt Library (Full Version) 114

Appendix B: Ethical Checklist & Consent Templates 141

Appendix C: Glossary of AI & Mental Health Terms 144

Appendix D: Resources & Further Reading 146

Chapter 1

Introduction to AI in Mental Health Practice

In the quiet hours after a full day of back-to-back sessions, a licensed clinical psychologist in private practice sits at her desk. She opens her secure, HIPAA-compliant platform, reviews a brief anonymized session summary she dictated earlier (no raw audio retained), and spends just five minutes refining an AI-generated DAP note. In another tab, she prompts a specialized tool for three evidence-based resource suggestions tailored to her client's current goals, carefully ensuring no protected health information ever leaves her compliant ecosystem. What used to take two hours of typing and formatting now takes under ten minutes, freeing her to reflect deeply on the therapeutic relationship rather than administrative drudgery.

This scene is no longer futuristic. In March 2026, thousands of mental health professionals, psychologists, counselors, clinical social workers, marriage and family therapists are integrating artificial intelligence into their daily workflows. They do so not to replace the irreplaceable human elements of therapy, but to reclaim time, reduce exhaustion, and refocus on what drew them to the field: genuine connection, empathy, and healing.

Yet alongside these successes come real cautions. Stories circulate in professional forums of clinicians who unwittingly entered session details into non-secure general-purpose AI tools, received fabricated or biased suggestions, or faced ethical scrutiny for insufficient transparency. The promise of AI in mental health is immense, but so are the risks if not approached with rigorous ethical and practical safeguards.

This book is written precisely for that purpose: to provide mental health professionals with a clear, ethics-first roadmap for using AI safely, compliantly, and effectively. Whether you're a solo practitioner feeling buried under notes, a clinic-based therapist seeking efficiency without compromising care, or simply curious about how tools like ChatGPT, Claude, or specialized platforms might fit into your work, this guide equips you with the knowledge to integrate AI as a thoughtful augmentor, never a substitute.

Why Now? The 2026 Landscape for Therapists

The mental health field faces unprecedented pressures. Demand for services has surged, with waitlists growing and access gaps widening in many communities. At the same time, providers themselves are straining under heavy loads. Recent surveys paint a stark picture of burnout:

- Therapists report spending approximately 35% of their working hours on documentation alone. In a typical week with 30 client sessions, that translates to more than eight hours just on notes and charting.
- Documentation and administrative burden rank as the top driver of burnout for mental health clinicians, cited by 23% of respondents in key 2025 surveys, and tying with low compensation as the leading factor.
- Overall, 77% of therapists experience significant mental fatigue,

the highest rate among healthcare specialties surveyed, with emotional and physical exhaustion close behind.

These numbers are not abstract. They reflect late nights charting, skipped self-care, and the creeping sense that paperwork is stealing time from clients and personal life.

Enter AI. Adoption has accelerated dramatically. According to the American Psychological Association's 2025 Practitioner Pulse Survey (with trends continuing into 2026):

- 56% of psychologists reported using AI tools at least once in their work, up sharply from prior years.
- 42% recognize AI's potential to reduce administrative burden and support practice operations, up 33% from the previous year.
- Specialized HIPAA-compliant tools designed for behavioral health (such as Twofold Health, Mentalyc, Upheal, AutoNotes, and others) have matured, offering accurate note generation, session analytics, and workflow automation while maintaining strict privacy standards.

The broader AI-in-healthcare surge supports this shift: domain-specific tools saw a 7x increase in implementation from 2024 to 2025 in some reports, with behavioral health following closely. In 2026, therapists who use AI ethically report reclaiming 5-10 hours per week, this is time that can translate to additional sessions, better self-care, or simply breathing room.

Myths vs. Reality: What AI Can (and Cannot) Do in Therapy

Myth 1: AI will replace human therapists.

Reality: AI excels at pattern recognition, summarization, and administrative support, but it lacks the embodied presence, relational depth, intuition, and ethical judgment that define effective therapy. The therapeutic alliance (the human-to-human bond) remains irreplaceable. AI augments; it does not supplant.

Myth 2: Any AI tool is fine as long as you're careful.

Reality: General-purpose large language models (like free or personal versions of ChatGPT, Claude, or Gemini) are powerful but not HIPAA-compliant without enterprise-level agreements and Business Associate Agreements (BAAs). Entering even anonymized session details risks breaches. Specialized tools with built-in compliance (e.g., Twofold Health for quick notes, Upheal for session insights, Mentalyc for audit-ready formats) are the safe path forward.

Myth 3: AI always gets it right.

Reality: Hallucinations, biases, and over-generalizations occur. Human oversight is non-negotiable, every AI output must be reviewed, edited, and validated against your clinical expertise.

Myth 4: Using AI means less personalized care.

Reality: When used correctly, AI frees cognitive bandwidth for deeper attunement, creative interventions, and personalized planning. Many clinicians report feeling more present with clients after offloading rote tasks.

Who This Book Is For, and What It Covers

This guide targets licensed mental health professionals in private practice, group practices, or agency settings who want practical, immediately applicable strategies. It assumes basic familiarity with therapy but no prior AI expertise.

Key focus areas include:

- Ethical frameworks from the APA's 2025-2026 guidance (emphasizing beneficence, nonmaleficence, transparency, bias mitigation, and human oversight).
- HIPAA and privacy essentials, including why general tools fall short and how compliant alternatives work.
- Tailored prompt engineering: crafting safe and effective inputs for therapy-specific tasks.
- Ready-to-adapt workflows for session prep, documentation (SOAP, DAP, BIRP), treatment planning, and resource creation.
- Tool comparisons and step-by-step implementation.
- Real-world case studies, burnout prevention, and forward-looking trends.

What this book does not do: It provides educational guidance only - not legal, clinical, or risk-management advice. Always consult your licensing board, malpractice carrier, HIPAA compliance expert, and professional associations before adopting any tool or workflow.

Your Path Forward

By the final chapter, you'll have a personalized playbook: vetted prompts, compliant tool recommendations, ethical checklists, and confidence to experiment without fear. You'll know how to start small (perhaps with anonymized note drafting), scale responsibly, and stay updated as the field evolves.

The integration of AI into mental health is not about technology overtaking humanity - it's about preserving humanity in therapy by removing barriers that drain providers. Turn the page to explore the ethical foundations that make responsible use possible.

Chapter 2
The Ethical Landscape: Guidelines, Risks, and Responsibilities

The integration of artificial intelligence into mental health practice is not merely a technical decision, it is fundamentally an ethical one. As therapists, our primary duty is to do no harm (nonmaleficence), to promote client welfare (beneficence), to respect autonomy, to uphold justice, and to maintain fidelity and integrity in all professional relationships. These core principles, drawn from longstanding ethical codes such as those of the American Psychological Association (APA) and the American Counseling Association (ACA), remain unchanged in the AI era. What has changed is the landscape in which we apply them.

In June 2025, the APA released its groundbreaking Ethical Guidance for AI in the Professional Practice of Health Service Psychology, a document specifically tailored to health service psychologists integrating AI into clinical settings. This guidance, updated through December 2025, emphasizes that AI must augment, not replace, human decision-making. Psychologists retain full responsibility for final judgments and must never blindly rely on AI outputs. The ACA, while its 2014 Code of Ethics does not yet explicitly address AI (with revisions anticipated to incorporate it), has issued practical recommendations through working groups, stressing informed consent, privacy compliance, and the irreplaceable value of human relationships in counseling.

This chapter explores the ethical foundations that must guide every AI interaction in therapy. We examine key principles from professional bodies, the primary risks that arise when these are overlooked, and practical responsibilities therapists bear to protect clients, maintain licensure integrity, and preserve the therapeutic alliance.

Core Ethical Principles in the AI Context

The APA's 2025 guidance aligns closely with its Ethical Principles of Psychologists and Code of Conduct (2017, with ongoing relevance), particularly:

- Principle A: Beneficence and Nonmaleficence - AI use must promote client welfare and avoid harm. This means rigorously evaluating tools for accuracy, bias, and potential negative impacts before adoption.
- Principle B: Fidelity and Responsibility - Therapists must maintain accountability for AI-assisted decisions, ensuring human oversight at every step.
- Principle C: Justice - AI should not exacerbate disparities; tools must be assessed for fairness across diverse populations.
- Principle D: Respect for People's Rights and Dignity - Transparency, informed consent, and efforts to mitigate bias are non-negotiable.

The ACA's recommendations echo these, emphasizing client empowerment, privacy under federal/state laws, and the need for counselors to stay informed about AI developments as part of ongoing professional competence (C.2.f in the 2014 Code).

Key shared imperatives include:

- Transparency and Informed Consent: Disclose AI use to clients (and relevant third parties, such as courts) in culturally and linguistically appropriate ways. Explain the purpose, benefits, limitations, and risks of any AI tool involved in their care.

- Human Oversight: AI outputs are advisory only. Therapists must review, edit, and validate every suggestion, note, or resource.

- Bias Mitigation and Equity: Evaluate tools for biases that could worsen health disparities. Strive to eliminate effects of bias on work, per Principle E.

- Professional Competence: Engage in continuing education on AI developments and ensure tools align with evidence-based behavioral health practices.

These principles are not optional, they form the guardrails that prevent AI from undermining the trust and safety essential to therapy.

Major Risks of AI in Psychotherapy

Despite AI's promise, real-world applications reveal significant hazards if ethical safeguards are absent. Recent studies and professional reports from 2025-2026 highlight recurring concerns:

1. Confidentiality and Privacy Breaches General-purpose large language models (e.g., free or personal versions of ChatGPT, Claude, or Gemini) lack inherent HIPAA compliance without enterprise-level Business Associate Agreements. Even anonymized inputs carry risks if data is inadvertently stored, shared, or used for model training. Specialized tools (e.g., those with built-in HIPAA safeguards) are safer, but therapists must verify compliance independently.

2. Hallucinations and Inaccurate Outputs AI can generate plausible but false information, fabricated diagnoses, unsupported interventions, or misleading summaries. A 2026 Brown University study found that even when prompted to emulate trained therapists, chatbots routinely violated ethical standards, including mishandling crises and producing deceptive empathy without genuine understanding.

3. Bias and Reinforcement of Harmful Beliefs Training data biases can lead to stigmatizing responses (e.g., toward schizophrenia or substance use disorders) or sycophantic reinforcement of a client's maladaptive views. The APA stresses evaluating tools to prevent exacerbation of disparities.

4. Over-Reliance and Erosion of Clinical Judgment Convenience can tempt therapists to accept AI suggestions without scrutiny, diminishing critical thinking and the nuanced attunement central to therapy.

5. Boundary Violations and Deceptive Empathy AI simulates compassion but lacks true relational depth, potentially creating

one-sided attachments or false senses of connection that harm vulnerable clients.

6. Crisis Mishandling In high-risk situations (e.g., suicidal ideation), AI may fail to escalate appropriately or provide inadequate safety planning.

These risks are not hypothetical, professional forums, surveys, and research (including APA's 2025 Practitioner Pulse data) show growing concerns about data privacy (top worry), bias, hallucinations, and social harms among psychologists using AI.

Therapist Responsibilities: Practical Guardrails

To navigate this landscape responsibly:

- Conduct Due Diligence on Tools - Use the APA's Companion Checklist for AI-Enabled Tools to assess quality, performance, bias, privacy features, and appropriateness for behavioral health.
- Obtain and Document Informed Consent - Update intake forms and treatment agreements to disclose AI use (e.g., "I may use HIPAA-compliant AI for note drafting or resource generation, with full human review").
- Maintain Rigorous Oversight - Adopt a "human-in-the-loop" rule: Review every output, edit for accuracy, and document rationale for changes.
- Protect Confidentiality - Never input identifiable PHI into non-compliant systems. Use anonymization or hypothetical sce-

narios when testing prompts.

- Monitor for Bias and Harm - Regularly audit AI suggestions against diverse client demographics and seek peer consultation on edge cases.
- Pursue Ongoing Education - Stay current via APA/ACA resources, webinars, and ethics committees. Treat AI literacy as part of professional competence.
- Consult When in Doubt - Discuss AI integration with malpractice carriers, licensing boards, or ethics hotlines before widespread adoption.

Moving Forward Ethically

Ethical AI use demands vigilance, humility, and a commitment to the human core of therapy. The APA and ACA guidance remind us that technology serves the profession, not the reverse. By grounding every decision in established principles, therapists can harness AI's efficiency while safeguarding the trust, safety, and dignity of those we serve.

The chapters ahead translate these foundations into concrete practices: crafting safe prompts, selecting compliant tools, and building workflows that honor both innovation and ethics.

Chapter 3

HIPAA, Privacy, and Data Security for AI Use

HIPAA , the Health Insurance Portability and Accountability Act of 1996, remains the cornerstone federal law governing the protection of protected health information (PHI) in the United States. For mental health professionals, HIPAA's Privacy Rule, Security Rule, and Breach Notification Rule impose strict requirements on how PHI is handled, stored, transmitted, and disclosed. In 2026, as AI tools become integral to practice workflows, understanding HIPAA compliance is non-negotiable. Failure to comply can result in significant fines (up to $50,000+ per violation, with annual caps in the millions), reputational damage, licensing issues, and most critically, harm to client trust.

This chapter breaks down HIPAA essentials for therapists, explains why general-purpose AI tools often fall short, highlights compliant alternatives that have matured by 2026, and provides actionable best practices to safeguard client data while leveraging AI for efficiency.

HIPAA Basics for Therapists

Under HIPAA, therapists in private practice or covered entities (e.g., those billing insurance) are "covered entities." Any vendor or tool that creates, receives, maintains, or transmits PHI on your behalf becomes a "business associate," requiring a signed Business Associate Agreement (BAA) that binds them to HIPAA standards.

Key elements include:

- Protected Health Information (PHI): Any individually identifiable health information (e.g., names, dates of service, diagnoses, session notes, treatment plans). Psychotherapy notes receive extra protection under the Privacy Rule as a separate category.
- Privacy Rule: Limits uses and disclosures of PHI; requires safeguards like minimum necessary access, client authorization for most releases, and rights to access/amend records.
- Security Rule: Mandates administrative, physical, and technical safeguards (e.g., encryption, access controls, audit logs, risk assessments).
- Breach Notification: Requires notification to affected individuals, HHS, and (in some cases) media if unsecured PHI is breached.

In 2026, no major overhaul has rewritten HIPAA for AI specifically, but enforcement has intensified around emerging tech. The HHS Office for Civil Rights (OCR) scrutinizes AI tools for unauthorized PHI exposure, data training on client info, and lack of BAAs. State laws (e.g., in Illinois, California) add layers, often requiring human review of AI outputs in therapy contexts.

Why General-Purpose LLMs Are Not HIPAA-Compliant (Without Safeguards)

Tools like free/personal ChatGPT, Claude, or Gemini excel at reasoning and prompt response but pose serious risks:

- No Standard BAA for Free/Personal Tiers: OpenAI, Anthropic, and Google offer BAAs only on enterprise/enterprise plans (e.g., ChatGPT Enterprise, Claude for Work). Free or standard accounts may use inputs for model training or store data insecurely.
- Data Retention and Training Risks: Inputs can persist in logs or be used to improve models unless explicitly opted out (and even then, enforcement varies).
- Transmission and Storage: Data travels unencrypted or through non-secure channels without proper controls.
- Auditability: Limited logs make breach detection or compliance audits difficult.

Real-world consequence: Even "anonymized" session summaries risk re-identification (e.g., unique phrasing + context). Therapists have faced complaints for accidental PHI exposure in non-compliant tools.

Compliant Alternatives: Specialized Tools for Mental Health in 2026

The market has matured significantly by 2026, with HIPAA-compliant AI platforms designed specifically for behavioral health. These offer signed

BAAs, no (or minimal) audio retention, encryption, audit trails, and therapy-focused features like DAP/SOAP/BIRP note generation, treatment planning, and session insights.

Top options based on 2026 clinician reviews, features, and compliance:

- Twofold Health - Frequently ranked #1 overall for behavioral health. Unlimited notes, zero audio retention post-processing, strong privacy filters (separates psychotherapy notes), SMART goal tracking, and flat-rate pricing (~$49/month annual). Excellent for private practices; praised for accuracy, EHR integration potential, and predictable costs.

- Mentalyc - Top for psychotherapy-specific accuracy and insights (e.g., sentiment analysis, progress tracking, Alliance Genie). Flexible templates (SOAP, DAP, BIRP, custom), no recordings stored, Chrome extension for EHR mapping. Pricing starts ~$15-$100/month (tiered by volume). Highly regarded for audit-ready notes and reducing edits.

- Upheal - Strong for session analytics and therapy-specific understanding (e.g., DAP notes, outcome tracking). HIPAA/SOC 2 compliant, but some plans involve recording (with consent). Pricing ~$19-$69/month. Good for clinicians wanting deeper insights, though the interface can feel complex.

- AutoNotes - Behavioral health-focused dictation to structured notes (SOAP/DAP/BIRP). HIPAA/PHIPA compliant, quick generation. Subscription-based; suits solo therapists but less social proof and integration depth compared to leaders.

- Other notables:

- Noted - Real-time transcription/integration with video tools.

- Freed AI / Supanote - Accurate clinical detail, multiple formats.

- SimplePractice Native AI - Built into a popular EHR for seamless workflow.

The Comparison Table on the next page features popular tools: Always verify current BAA, privacy policy, and reviews before signing up, compliance can evolve.

AI Tools for Therapists — Comparison Table (2026)

Best Practices: Anonymization, Workflows, and Risk Mitigation

1. Never Enter Real PHI in Non-Compliant Tools - Use hypotheticals or fully de-identified summaries (remove 18 identifiers per HIPAA).

2. Anonymization Techniques - Replace names with placeholders (e.g., "Client A"), generalize ages/dates, avoid unique details.

3. Secure Workflows - Dictate via compliant apps - generate drafts - human review/edit - finalize in EHR. Use secure dictation if recording.

4. Informed Consent & Disclosure - Update forms: "I use HIPAA-compliant AI for note drafting/resource generation, with full review."

5. Regular Risk Assessments - Conduct annual HIPAA security risk analysis; include AI tools.

6. Audit & Documentation - Log AI use; retain versions of edited notes.

7. Client Rights - Honor access/amendment requests; explain AI role transparently.

Final Thoughts

HIPAA compliance isn't optional, it's the foundation for ethical AI use. By choosing BAA-signed, behavioral-health-specific tools and maintaining rigorous safeguards, therapists can safely harness AI to reduce burden without risking client privacy or professional integrity.

The next chapters shift to practical application: mastering prompt engineering within these compliant boundaries.

Chapter 4

Prompt Engineering Basics - From Beginner to Advanced

Prompt engineering is the art and science of crafting precise, effective inputs (prompts) to guide large language models (LLMs) toward producing accurate, useful, and safe outputs. For therapists, this skill is essential because generic prompts often yield vague, robotic, or even inappropriate responses, while well-engineered ones can generate thoughtful session outlines, note drafts, resource ideas, or self-reflection questions that align closely with ethical, evidence-based practice.

In 2026, models like ChatGPT (Enterprise), Claude, Gemini, and specialized behavioral health tools have become remarkably capable, but their performance still hinges on how clearly you communicate intent. Poor prompts lead to hallucinations, irrelevant tangents, or outputs that ignore ethical boundaries. Strong prompts produce focused, professional results with minimal editing.

This chapter starts with foundational concepts for beginners (no prior AI experience required) then progresses to intermediate and advanced techniques tailored to therapy workflows. All examples emphasize safety: anonymization, role constraints, and ethical guardrails to prevent misuse.

What Is Prompt Engineering?

At its core, prompt engineering is natural-language programming. Instead of writing code, you write instructions in plain English (or your preferred language) that direct the model's reasoning and output. Effective prompts act like clear contracts: they define expectations, reduce ambiguity, and steer the model away from undesirable behaviors.

Key benefits for therapists:

- Save time on repetitive tasks (e.g., brainstorming interventions).
- Generate structured, editable drafts (notes, handouts).
- Maintain consistency in tone (empathetic, professional, non-diagnostic).

Common pitfalls to avoid early:

- Vague language - vague outputs.
- Including real PHI - privacy risks (always anonymize).
- No constraints - overly creative or off-topic responses.

Basic Structure of an Effective Prompt

A strong prompt typically includes five core components (often summarized as Role + Task + Context + Format + Constraints):

1. Role/Persona - Assign the model a specific identity to shape its perspective and tone. Example: "You are an experienced, ethical clinical assistant trained in CBT and ACT principles."
2. Task/Instruction - Clearly state what you want done. Use action

verbs. Example: "Generate a session agenda outline for the next appointment."

3. Context - Provide necessary background (anonymized client summary, session goals, modality). Example: "The client is a 35-year-old professional experiencing generalized anxiety. Last session focused on worry monitoring; they reported partial success with diaphragmatic breathing."

4. Format/Output Structure - Specify how the response should be organized (e.g., bullet points, numbered steps, sections). Example: "Structure your response with: 1) Opening check-in questions, 2) Core activities, 3) Homework suggestions, 4) Potential pitfalls."

5. Constraints/Limitations - Set boundaries to ensure safety and relevance. Example: "Do not diagnose, prescribe, or provide therapeutic advice. Use only evidence-based suggestions. Respond only as a supportive assistant, never as a licensed therapist."

Beginner Example Prompt (Full Template):

You are an ethical clinical assistant with expertise in cognitive behavioral therapy. Never diagnose, never give direct therapeutic advice, and always remind that outputs need human review.

Task: Create a brief, anonymized session planning outline.

Context: Client (anonymized): Adult with social anxiety. Previous focus: Exposure hierarchy building. They completed one small exposure last week but felt overwhelmed.

Format: Use bullet points with these sections:

- Suggested check-in questions

- Main intervention ideas

- Homework options

- Ethical notes/reminders

Constraints: Keep suggestions general and evidence-based. Limit to 300 words. End with: "Review and adapt this with your clinical judgment."

Run this in a compliant tool - get a focused, usable outline.

Intermediate Techniques: Building on Basics

Once comfortable with structure, layer these enhancements:

Few-Shot Prompting - Provide 1-3 examples of desired input-output pairs to "teach" the model your preferred style.

Example addition:

"Example 1:

Input: Client with low mood, recent job loss.

Output: [structured agenda example]

- Now apply the same format to this new context..." This improves consistency for recurring tasks like note formatting.

Chain-of-Thought (CoT) Prompting - Instruct the model to "think step by step" for better reasoning on complex tasks (e.g., hypothesizing intervention sequences).

- Example: "Let's think step by step: First, review the presenting concern. Second, recall relevant CBT principles. Third, propose matched interventions. Finally, outline the session." In 2026, many models support "reasoning effort" parameters (Low/Med/High) to control internal CoT depth, (use Medium for therapy planning).

Role-Playing with Constraints - Deepen persona for nuanced tone.

- Example: "You are a compassionate, non-judgmental clinical consultant specializing in trauma-informed care. Always prioritize safety and empowerment."

Advanced Techniques for Therapy-Specific Use

- Iterative Refinement - Start broad, then refine based on output. First prompt: Generate ideas. Follow-up: "Revise the above to be more trauma-sensitive, removing any exposure elements."

- Self-Consistency / Multiple Paths - Generate 3-5 variations, then select the best and combine. Useful for brainstorming resources.

- Ethical Guardrail Prompts - Embed rules repeatedly: "Throughout your response, adhere strictly to: No PHI assumptions, no diagnosis, flag any potentially harmful suggestion, emphasize human oversight."

- Zero-Shot CoT for Quick Tasks - For simple reasoning: Add "Let's think step by step" without examples.

Therapy-Tailored Advanced Example (Note Summarization Prep):

You are a HIPAA-compliant clinical documentation assistant. Your role is to help outline anonymized progress notes only - never create final clinical records.

Task: From this anonymized session summary, generate a draft DAP note structure.

Context: Session 8. Client discussed increased panic attacks at work. Used grounding techniques with moderate success. Mood improved slightly by end.

Step-by-step reasoning: 1) Identify key data points. 2) Organize into Data, Assessment, Plan. 3) Ensure language remains objective and non-diagnostic.

Format:

- Data: [bullet points of observations/content]

- Assessment: [therapist's clinical impressions - keep neutral]

- Plan: [next steps, homework]

Constraints: Limit to 250 words. Use only information provided. Remind: "This is a draft for your review and editing only. Do not enter real PHI."

Common Mistakes and Fixes

- Mistake: Too vague ("Help with notes"). Fix: Add role, format, constraints.
- Mistake: Overloading context. Fix: Keep under 1,000-2,000 tokens; summarize.
- Mistake: Ignoring model differences. Fix: Test in your tool (Claude excels at long reasoning; Gemini at structured output).

Practice Exercises

1. Beginner: Write a basic prompt for generating psychoeducation bullet points on mindfulness.
2. Intermediate: Add few-shot examples for consistent handout style.
3. Advanced: Build a CoT prompt for hypothesizing relational patterns from anonymized summaries.

Mastering these basics unlocks the prompt libraries in Chapter 6. Practice iteratively in your compliant tool - small refinements yield big improvements in efficiency and safety.

Chapter 5

Building Safe, Effective Prompts - Core Principles for Therapists

With the foundational structure of prompt engineering in place from Chapter 4, this chapter focuses on the therapist-specific adaptations that make prompts truly safe, clinically appropriate, and useful in real practice. The goal is not just to get good outputs, but to get outputs that respect ethical boundaries, minimize risk, reduce editing time, and align with evidence-based principles, while always preserving your role as the final clinical decision-maker.

In 2026, even the most advanced models can produce outputs that sound convincingly professional yet contain subtle errors: over-diagnosis language, inappropriate intervention suggestions, boundary-crossing empathy simulation, or assumptions about client identity. The principles in this chapter are designed to create a "safety net" around every prompt you write or reuse.

We'll cover seven core principles for therapists, explain why each matters, provide practical rules-of-thumb, and demonstrate them through before-and-after examples. By the end, you'll have a reusable checklist you can apply to any prompt.

Core Principle 1: Always Explicitly Define the Role and Its Limits

Never let the model assume it is a therapist. Assign a narrow, supportive role (e.g., clinical assistant, documentation aide, resource brainstormer) and repeat prohibitions.

Why it matters: Models trained on vast internet data often default to "helpful therapist" personas, which can lead to diagnostic language, direct advice, or simulated therapeutic dialogue.

Rule-of-thumb: Start every prompt with a clear role statement + "never" list.

Bad example (risky):

"Write a progress note for this session summary."

Good example (safe):

"You are an ethical clinical documentation assistant. You do NOT diagnose, do NOT provide therapeutic advice, do NOT simulate empathy or therapeutic dialogue, and do NOT act as a licensed mental health professional. Your role is ONLY to help organize anonymized information into structured note formats for human review."

Core Principle 2: Mandate Anonymization and Zero PHI

Even "anonymized" details can sometimes be re-identifiable. Force the model to treat all input as hypothetical and strip identifiers.

Why it matters: Protects against accidental breaches if outputs are saved, shared, or audited.

Rule-of-thumb: Include: "Treat all information in this prompt as fully hypothetical and anonymized. Do not assume or invent any real names, dates, locations, or identifying details."

Before:

"Client is a 42-year-old woman from Florida with depression after job loss."

After (safer):

"Hypothetical adult client experiencing low mood following employment change. No names, locations, or specific identifiers are provided or to be used."

Core Principle 3: Enforce Evidence-Based, Modality-Specific Boundaries

Tie suggestions to recognized therapeutic frameworks and exclude unsupported or fringe approaches.

Why it matters: Prevents the model from pulling outdated, pseudoscientific, or harmful ideas from training data.

Rule-of-thumb: Specify accepted modalities (e.g., "Draw only from CBT, DBT, ACT, solution-focused, trauma-informed care, motivational interviewing, and mindfulness-based approaches recognized by APA/ACA.")

Example addition:

"Base all suggestions strictly on evidence-based practices from CBT, ACT, and mindfulness-based interventions. Do not suggest unproven methods, supplements, or alternative therapies."

Core Principle 4: Require Step-by-Step Reasoning and Self-Check

Instruct the model to show its work and self-evaluate against ethical criteria.

Why it matters: Chain-of-thought improves accuracy and makes it easier for you to spot flawed logic.

Rule-of-thumb: Add: "Think step by step: 1) Review the input. 2) Recall relevant ethical guidelines. 3) Apply only appropriate techniques. 4) Flag any potential concern. 5) Output the final response."

Core Principle 5: Specify Output Format Rigorously

Therapists need consistency, structured formats reduce editing time and errors.

Why it matters: Free-form responses waste time reformatting.

Rule-of-thumb: Always dictate exact sections, headings, bullet styles, word limits, and tone.

Example:

"Output ONLY in this exact structure:

1. Suggested Check-In Questions (3-5 bullets)

2. Potential Interventions (evidence-based only, 3-4 bullets)

3. Homework Ideas (2-3 realistic options)
4. Ethical Reminders (2-3 bullets) Keep total under 400 words. Use professional, neutral, non-diagnostic language."

Core Principle 6: Embed Human Oversight and Review Reminders

Force the model to remind you (and itself) that the output is advisory only.

Why it matters: Reinforces your responsibility and creates a paper trail of caution.

Rule-of-thumb: End every prompt with: "End your response with this exact sentence: 'This is a draft suggestion only. Review thoroughly, edit as needed, and apply your clinical judgment before use.'"

Core Principle 7: Use Iterative Safeguards and Version Control

Build prompts that encourage refinement and versioning.

Why it matters: First drafts are rarely perfect; iteration catches issues.

Rule-of-thumb: After initial output, follow up with:

"Review your previous response for: 1) Any diagnostic language, 2) Any boundary-crossing statements, 3) Any non-evidence-based suggestions. Revise if needed and explain changes."

Putting It All Together: Full Safe Prompt Template for Therapists

Here is a reusable master template you can copy and adapt:

You are an ethical clinical support assistant specialized in behavioral health documentation and planning. You are NOT a licensed therapist. You do NOT diagnose, do NOT provide therapy, do NOT simulate therapeutic relationships, and do NOT offer direct clinical advice.

Rules you MUST follow at all times:

- Treat all client information as fully hypothetical and anonymized. Never use, assume, or invent real names, dates, locations, or identifiers.

- Draw suggestions ONLY from evidence-based modalities: CBT, DBT, ACT, solution-focused, motivational interviewing, trauma-informed care, mindfulness-based approaches.

- Never suggest medication, supplements, unproven therapies, or crisis interventions without clear escalation language.

- Flag any output that could be misinterpreted as diagnostic or directive.

- Keep language objective, professional, and neutral.

Task: [insert specific task, e.g., Generate a session planning outline]

Context: [insert anonymized, hypothetical summary]

Format: [insert exact structure]

Now think step by step:

1. Review the context and task.

2. Recall relevant ethical and evidence-based guidelines.

3. Apply only appropriate, safe suggestions.

4. Check for any potential ethical concern.

5. Produce the final output.

End your response with this exact sentence: "This is a draft suggestion only. Review thoroughly, edit as needed, and apply your clinical judgment before use."

Quick Checklist for Every Prompt You Write

Before hitting enter:

- Role and prohibitions clearly stated?
- All info treated as hypothetical/anonymized?
- Modality boundaries specified?
- Step-by-step reasoning requested?
- Output format rigidly defined?
- Human oversight reminder included?
- Word limit or brevity constraint?

Master these principles, and your prompts will consistently produce outputs that are faster to review, safer to use, and more aligned with professional standards. The next chapter builds on this foundation with a ready-to-copy library of 100+ vetted, profession-specific prompts organized by workflow stage.

Chapter 6

Working With the Prompt Library - A Category-by-Category Workflow Guide

There is a difference between having a tool and knowing how to use it.

The prompt library in Appendix A contains 60 complete, copy-paste-ready prompts organized across six workflow categories. Every one of them has been engineered with the safety principles from Chapter 5. Each prompt has explicit role limits, mandatory anonymization, evidence-based constraints, step-by-step reasoning, and human oversight reminders built in. They are ready to use today.

But a library, however well-stocked, only serves you if you know which shelf to reach for. A therapist sitting down after a long day of sessions, facing a stack of notes and a blank screen, does not need more information. She needs to know exactly which prompt to open, why it fits this moment, and what to watch for when the output comes back.

That is what this chapter gives you.

We will walk through all six prompt categories, not as an index, but as a workflow guide. For each category you will learn when to reach for it, what clinical situations call for it, how to choose between the variants available in the library, what the common pitfalls are, and how to read the output intelligently. One fully annotated example in each category will show you not just what a good prompt looks like, but why each element is there and what happens when you leave something out.

By the end of this chapter, the library in Appendix A will feel less like a reference document and more like a set of tools you already know how to use.

Three principles apply across all six categories before we begin.

Every prompt is a starting point, not a final product.

The prompts in Appendix A are engineered to produce high-quality outputs, but they are built for hypothetical contexts. Your job is to bring clinical reality to them, replacing the placeholders with the actual anonymized specifics of your situation, adjusting the modality if your client works in a different framework, and trusting your own clinical judgment to catch anything the output gets wrong.

The platform matters as much as the prompt.

A perfect prompt run in a non-HIPAA-compliant tool is a compliance risk. Before you use any prompt from this library with client-adjacent information, confirm your tool has a signed Business Associate Agreement and meets the standards described in Chapter 3.

Refinement is the practice.

Most therapists who integrate AI successfully describe a learning curve of roughly three to six weeks during which they are actively refining their prompts, noticing what produces too much text, what misses clinical nuance, and what gets the format exactly right. The prompts in Appendix A are the floor, not the ceiling. The guidance at the end of this chapter on building your personal prompt library will show you how to get there.

Category 1: Session Preparation and Planning (Prompts 1-14)

When to reach for this category:

Any time you are preparing for an upcoming session and want structured scaffolding for your planning. This includes routine weekly sessions where you want to ensure clinical coherence, complex cases where you are managing multiple treatment threads simultaneously, transitions, new treatment phases, termination, or a client returning after a break.

What this category does well:

Session prep prompts excel at organizing what you already know about a case into a usable clinical structure. They are pattern-recognition engines. When you paste in an anonymized summary of recent sessions, the model identifies the therapeutic threads, aligns them with the framework you have specified, and produces an agenda that reflects sound clinical logic. You still bring the relationship, the attunement, the intuitive read of what this client needs today. The prompt handles the scaffolding.

What this category cannot do:

It cannot know what happened in your last session the way you experienced it. It cannot feel the rupture that formed when you said something that landed wrong in week nine. It cannot read the quality of the silence that told you the client was ready to go deeper. Whatever the prompt produces is an informed suggestion based on the information you provided, and you provided it in summary form, stripped of the relational texture that defines your actual clinical knowledge.

Choosing between the variants:

Appendix A contains 14 session prep prompts. For standard adult individual sessions, Prompts 1, 5, and 13 cover CBT, intake, and ACT respectively. For trauma-informed work, Prompt 2 is specifically built for the stabilization phase with a window of tolerance considerations embedded. Prompt 3 for adolescent DBT. Prompt 4 for couples. When you are preparing for a session with a client whose cultural background differs significantly from your own, Prompt 12 on cultural considerations belongs in your pre-session routine. For crisis follow-up sessions, Prompt 7 builds in safety assessment scaffolding that Prompt 1 does not.

Annotated Example - Prompt 1, Basic Session Agenda:

You are an ethical clinical planning assistant. You do NOT diagnose, provide therapy, or act as a licensed professional. Treat all information as fully hypothetical. The role definition does three things simultaneously: assigns a specific narrow identity (planning assistant, not therapist), explicitly prohibits the behaviors most likely to produce inappropriate outputs (diagnosis, therapy, licensure claims), and instructs the model to treat all content as hypothetical. Remove any of these three and output quality degrades in predictable ways. Task: Generate a session agenda for an upcoming appointment. Context: Hypothetical adult client working on generalized anxiety. Last session: cognitive restructuring. Homework: thought record, partial compliance. Format: - Check-in questions (4, open-ended) - Homework review approach - Main intervention (1-2 CBT techniques)

- Closing and new homework - Therapist self-care reminder Constraints: CBT only. Max 350 words. Think step by step. The context contains the two pieces of information that most shape agenda design, the treatment framework (CBT) and the homework status (partial compliance, which means the agenda needs to address non-completion without shaming). Without the word count limit, AI outputs often run long. "Think step by step" activates chain-of-thought reasoning, which meaningfully improves clinical logic in the output. End with: "This is a draft suggestion only. Review thoroughly, edit as needed, and apply your clinical judgment before use." This line is required at the end of every session prep prompt. It reinforces the human-in-the-loop principle at the moment of output, it is literally the last thing the model produces before you read its work.

When the output returns, read it once as a skeptic. Ask: does this reflect what I know about this client, or is it a generic anxiety agenda? Does the homework review section actually address the partial compliance pattern? Is the intervention one I would genuinely choose? Edit accordingly. The output should take seven to ten minutes to review and refine, not thirty seconds to accept and move on.

Category 2: Progress Notes and Documentation (Prompts 15-27)

When to reach for this category:

Immediately after sessions, while your memory is still fresh and the clinical detail is still available. Documentation prompts work best when you spend three to five minutes writing anonymized bullet points right after the session ends and feed those bullets into the prompt. This workflow (rapid bullets then AI draft) is where the largest time savings live. Most therapists who integrate AI documentation report reducing per-note time from forty-five minutes down to eight to fifteen minutes. The quality of your bullets is the primary driver of the quality of the output.

What this category does well:

Structural organization. AI is genuinely excellent at taking a list of clinical observations and organizing them into the correct format - DAP, SOAP, BIRP, GIRP - with appropriate language in each section. It maintains the distinction between Data and Assessment that many therapists find difficult to write cleanly under time pressure. It also flags when your bullets contain more assessment language than data language, which is a valuable quality-control function.

What this category cannot do:

Add clinical nuance you did not provide. If your bullet points are thin, the output will be thin. The AI cannot reconstruct what you observed from a vague summary. This is actually a feature rather than a limitation: documentation prompts hold you accountable for the quality of your clinical observations. If your bullets are specific, the notes will be specific.

Choosing the right note format:

This is a clinical decision, not a prompt selection decision. Choose your format based on your setting, payer requirements, and theoretical orientation, then select the matching prompt. Prompts 15 through 18 cover DAP, SOAP, BIRP, and GIRP for general adult outpatient work. Prompt 19 is EMDR-specific. Prompt 20 handles group therapy documentation with member privacy protections built in. Prompt 21 is the crisis documentation prompt, use it after any session involving acute risk. It produces documentation that is more legally defensible because it requires you to document your risk assessment tool, risk level, safety plan status, and follow-up timeline explicitly.

Annotated Example - Prompt 15, DAP Note:

You are a HIPAA-compliant documentation assistant. You NEVER create final records, NEVER diagnose, and NEVER include uninvited details. "Never include uninvited details" directly addresses hallucination risk in documentation context. AI models sometimes add clinical observations or interpretations that were not in your source material. This phrasing makes fabrication a rule violation, not just a quality issue. Context: Hypothetical session. Client discussed work deadline stress. Identified cognitive distortion: catastrophizing. Practiced thought challenging. Mood: 6/10 start, 7/10 end. No safety concerns. Homework: thought record for one stressor this week. Observe the specifics: mood ratings, the named distortion, the intervention, the homework. These specifics allow the AI to write a specific note rather than a generic one. "Client worked on cognitive distortions and reported improved mood" produces a different, and far less clinically useful, output. Constraints: Objective language. Max 250 words. No invented details. Think step by step. "Neutral" in the Assessment section keeps clinical impressions in the appropriate register - observable change and progress, not pathology framing. Without this constraint the model may slip into language that reads like diagnostic opinion.

Every documentation output deserves two passes before entering your EHR. First pass - accuracy: does this note reflect what actually happened? Check every specific claim. Second pass - language: does it reflect your professional voice and judgment? The note will carry your signature. It should sound like you.

Category 3: Treatment Planning and Goal Setting (Prompts 28-34)

When to reach for this category:

When beginning treatment and drafting initial goals, when conducting treatment plan reviews and updating goals mid-treatment, when a client has met an existing goal and you need to articulate the next one, and when developing relapse prevention plans as treatment nears completion.

What this category does well:

SMART goal generation and treatment framework alignment. Writing goals that are genuinely Specific, Measurable, Achievable, Relevant, and Time-bound is harder than it sounds under clinical time pressure. Most therapists know what they want the goal to express but struggle to translate clinical intent into SMART language. Prompts 28 through 33 do that translation reliably.

What this category cannot do:

Determine the right treatment direction. The prompts generate goals within the framework you specify, but the clinical judgment about which direction serves this client is entirely yours. If you are uncertain about the right treatment approach, a treatment planning prompt will not resolve that uncertainty - it may produce a plausible-sounding goal that is clinically wrong for this client. Know your clinical direction before reaching for this category.

Choosing between the variants:

Prompt 28 generates initial goal options for anxiety. Prompt 29 is relapse prevention, appropriate when treatment is successful and termination is approaching. Prompt 30 generates ACT values clarification activities. Prompt 31 is behavioral activation planning for depression. Prompt 32 produces a Safety Plan framework in Stanley-Brown format, use this as a structural template and fill it in collaboratively with the client; never generate a safety plan without direct client involvement. Prompt 34 is the phased treatment plan for complex trauma.

Annotated Example - Prompt 28, SMART Goal Brainstorm:

Context: Hypothetical adult client. Social anxiety interfering with work presentations. Avoidance is the primary maintaining factor. The context names the maintaining factor explicitly: avoidance. This directs the model toward exposure-based goal language rather than insight-based language. If your formulation of the maintaining factor is accurate, the prompt will generate goals that address the right mechanism. The prompt cannot validate your formulation. It can only work within it. Constraints: No diagnostic assumptions. Client-centered language. Exposure approaches must include gradual hierarchy. The constraint about gradual hierarchy is a safety guardrail. Without it, the model might generate a goal that implies full exposure without preparation. It is technically correct but clinically inappropriate. Adding modality-specific safety constraints to treatment planning prompts is a habit worth building.

Category 4: Client Resources and Psychoeducation (Prompts 35-44)

When to reach for this category:

Whenever you want to give a client something tangible to take away from a session, a handout explaining a concept you just introduced, a worksheet to practice a skill between appointments, a reference sheet for a technique they found helpful. Before AI, creating these materials meant pulling from a generic library that may not match your theoretical approach or spending twenty minutes writing from scratch. Now it takes five minutes to generate a draft and ten minutes to personalize it.

What this category does well:

Clear, structured, accessible psychoeducation content. The prompts produce materials at approximately an eighth-grade reading level. The material is accessible to most adults without being condescending, appropriate for clients from a range of educational backgrounds, and genuinely evidence-based rather than pop psychology.

The personalization imperative:

Client-facing materials require more personalization than any other prompt category. Before giving any AI-generated material to a client you must: read it in full with that specific client in mind, adjust the reading level if needed, add a personal note connecting it to your session work, remove anything that does not fit, put your name and practice information on it, and deliver it through a secure HIPAA-compliant channel. A client who receives a handout you have clearly adapted to the work you are doing together will feel seen. That connection is worth the ten minutes.

What to never do in this category:

Never use an AI-generated resource for clients in crisis, clients with active psychosis or paranoia about technology, clients who have explicitly requested no AI involvement in their care, or any situation involving safety planning. These materials are educational supplements, not crisis supports, and framing them as such creates dangerous over-reliance.

Annotated Example - Prompt 37, Grounding Techniques:

Context: General adult audience, anxiety or dissociation. Notice that the context is general rather than client-specific. This is intentional and required. You are generating educational content, not clinical material tailored to a diagnosed client. The moment you add identifying or diagnostic information to a client resource prompt, you have moved into territory that requires different oversight. End with: "These are general skills only. Contact your therapist or a crisis line if you are in distress or unsafe." The required safety note is non-negotiable in this category. Client-facing materials must always redirect to professional or crisis support for anything beyond general skill practice. This protects both the client and your practice.

Category 5: Between-Session and Homework Support (Prompts 45-50)

When to reach for this category:

When you want to send a brief message through your secure client portal between sessions to acknowledge a client's effort on a homework assignment, to send a gentle reminder, or to provide a take-home skill reference. This category has the fewest prompts for good reason: between-session contact must stay in a narrow, well-defined lane.

The ethical boundaries of this category are strict.

Review Chapter 9 before using any of these prompts. Between-session AI use must never simulate therapeutic interaction, ask clinical questions, or serve as a substitute for a session. The messages generated by these prompts are warm, brief, non-therapeutic communications that your client receives with your name on them. They are the professional equivalent of a brief note a doctor might leave for a patient. They are informational and supportive, never clinical.

What this category does well:

Consistent, professional between-session communication that maintains the therapeutic relationship without breaching the session boundary. Many therapists struggle with between-session contact, either avoiding it because personalized messages take too long, or overdoing it in ways that blur boundaries. These prompts produce the right register: warm but not intimate, supportive but not therapeutic, brief but not cold.

Annotated Example - Prompt 45, Between-Session Check-In:

Format: 2-4 sentences. Warm but professional. Acknowledge effort without clinical interpretation. Does not require response. "Acknowledge effort without clinical interpretation" is the line between a supportive message and a clinical one. "That took courage and I know it was not easy" acknowledges effort. "This suggests your avoidance hierarchy is progressing as expected" is the clinical interpretation. The first is appropriate. The second is not. "Does not require response" shapes the entire tone. A message that implicitly expects a reply pulls the client toward between-session therapeutic interaction.

Category 6: Therapist Self-Care and Reflection (Prompts 51-60)

When to reach for this category:

After difficult sessions, at the end of heavy clinical days, in the quiet moment before supervision when you want to organize your thinking, and periodically as a professional wellness check-in. (The way a good clinician checks in with their clients about wellbeing between treatment phases).

This category is the one most likely to be skipped, and it may be the one that matters most.

The research on therapist burnout is clear on one point: the most effective protection against compassion fatigue is not resilience, it is structured reflection. Therapists who build regular practices of professional self-examination, peer consultation, and intentional self-care show lower burnout rates, stronger therapeutic alliances, and better clinical outcomes than those who push through on willpower alone. You cannot give from an empty vessel, and this category exists to help you maintain yours.

What this category does well:

Structured prompts for experiences that therapists often process inadequately, or not at all. The after-session debrief when you saw something that shook you. The countertransference you noticed but did not examine. The quiet accumulation of vicarious trauma you are carrying without fully realizing it. These prompts do not replace personal therapy, supervision, or peer consultation. What they provide is an accessible, immediate structure for reflection that costs five minutes and may prevent weeks of unexamined accumulation.

An important clarification:

The outputs from this category are for your personal reflection only. They are not clinical documentation. Do not save them in client files. Do not share them with supervisors as documentation of your oversight process.

They are the professional equivalent of a private journal. They are tools for self-awareness, not records.

Choosing between the variants:

Prompt 51 is the go-to immediately after a heavy session, designed to run in the five minutes before your next client. Prompt 52 explores countertransference when you have noticed a reaction and want to examine it before supervision. Prompt 53 is the quarterly burnout self-assessment. Set a calendar reminder and use it four times a year. Prompt 54 is weekly intention-setting, a two-minute practice that a surprising number of therapists find orienting before a clinical week begins. Prompt 55 is the between-sessions reset, specifically designed for the gap between a high-intensity session and whatever comes next.

Annotated Example - Prompt 51, Post-Session Debrief:

You are a reflective practice assistant for licensed therapists only. You support therapist processing - not client analysis. "Not client analysis" is the core ethical boundary of this entire category. The model's job is to help you process your experience, not to formulate the client, interpret client dynamics, or generate hypotheses about what the client's presentation means. If your outputs in this category contain clinical observations about the client rather than reflective questions about your own experience, your context was too client-focused. Rewrite it with yourself as the subject. End with: "This reflection is for your personal processing only. It is not clinical documentation." The closing reminder in this category is different from all the others. It does not say "review and edit." It says this is personal and is not documentation. That distinction matters for how you store it, how you relate to the material, and the professional boundaries it reinforces.

Building Your Personal Prompt Library

The 60 prompts in Appendix A will serve you well. The prompts you develop from refining them over six months of active clinical use will serve you better.

Every therapist who integrates AI successfully eventually builds a personal prompt library. It is a document that lives in their EHR or an encrypted notes application and contains their most reliable, refined prompts annotated with notes about when to use them. This library typically begins with three to five prompts from Appendix A that get used repeatedly, refined iteration by iteration until the outputs require minimal editing.

Here is how to build yours deliberately.

Begin with one category. Documentation is usually the best starting point because the return on investment is immediate and the feedback loop is tight. Use Prompt 15 for every session this week. After each use, note: what did the output get right, what did it get wrong, and what change to the prompt would have prevented the error? After five sessions, make those changes. The revised prompt is now yours.

After four weeks in documentation, add one session prep prompt to your rotation. After another four weeks, add one resource generation prompt. By the end of three months you will have a working personal library of eight to twelve highly refined prompts that produce outputs you trust. Adopt a habit of continuous improvement that keeps that library current.

Keep a simple log: prompt name, date used, time saved, editing required, and notes for refinement. After six months, review the log. You will find two or three prompts that consistently perform and two or three that consistently disappoint. Retire the disappointers. Promote the performers.

This is how a professional tool becomes a professional practice.

The next four chapters apply these categories to full daily workflows. Session preparation in Chapter 7, documentation in Chapter 8, in-session and between-session boundaries in Chapter 9, and client-facing resources in Chapter 10. The library in Appendix A will feel increasingly familiar as you move through them.

Chapter 7

AI-Assisted Session Preparation and Planning

Session preparation is where many therapists reclaim the most immediate value from AI. In a typical week, you might spend 30-60 minutes per client reviewing notes, reflecting on progress, brainstorming interventions, and outlining an agenda, all before the session even begins. By March 2026, compliant AI tools and carefully engineered prompts can cut this time in half or more, allowing deeper attunement to the client's needs rather than scrambling through files.

This chapter focuses exclusively on pre-session uses: agenda outlining, hypothesis generation, intervention brainstorming, resource selection, and potential obstacle anticipation. All activities occur

before the session starts, using only anonymized, hypothetical, or past-session summaries (never live or real-time PHI). This keeps everything firmly within ethical and HIPAA-safe boundaries, no audio recording, no in-session AI listening, no direct client interaction via AI.

We'll cover:

- Why pre-session prep is the safest entry point for AI.
- Step-by-step workflows using prompts from Chapter 6.

- Tool integration tips (e.g., Twofold Health, Mentalyc, or general compliant LLMs with BAA).
- Real-world examples and common pitfalls.
- Ethical checkpoints to maintain human-centered care.

Why Pre-Session Preparation Is the Ideal Starting Point for AI

Pre-session work involves low-risk, high-reward tasks: organizing thoughts, generating ideas, and planning structure. Unlike note-taking (post-session) or in-session support, it avoids:

- Real-time PHI exposure.
- Dependency on live transcription accuracy.
- Risk of AI influencing the therapeutic moment directly.

Therapists report that AI excels here because it handles pattern recognition and idea generation quickly, freeing cognitive space for empathy, intuition, and relational nuance, the elements no model can replicate.

In 2026, tools like Berries AI (which suggests treatment plan elements and session prep summaries), Mentalyc (with progress-tracking insights), and Twofold Health (unlimited note-related brainstorming) support this phase. Even general compliant LLMs (ChatGPT Enterprise, Claude for Work) work well if you stick to anonymized inputs.

Key ethical alignment (per APA 2025 guidance):

- Human oversight remains 100%.
- Outputs are advisory drafts only.
- No client-facing AI use without explicit disclosure and consent.

Core Pre-Session Workflow Using AI

Standard 5-step process (adaptable to 15-30 minutes per client):

1. Review Past Notes/Anonymized Summary - Pull key themes from your EHR or previous AI-drafted notes (no new PHI entry).
2. Prompt for Agenda Outline - Use a structured prompt to generate a draft agenda.
3. Brainstorm Interventions & Hypotheses - Generate modality-specific ideas.
4. Anticipate Obstacles & Contingencies - Flag potential challenges.
5. Finalize & Personalize - Review, edit, and integrate your clinical judgment.

Example 1: Full Pre-Session Agenda Prompt (CBT-Focused Adult Client)

Copy-paste ready (drawn from Appendix A and enhanced for pre-session use):

You are an ethical clinical planning assistant specialized in CBT. You do NOT diagnose, do NOT provide therapy, do NOT act as a licensed therapist. Treat all information as fully hypothetical and anonymous.

Task: Generate a complete pre-session agenda outline for the upcoming appointment.

Context: Hypothetical adult client addressing generalized anxiety. From prior sessions: Client has been tracking worry thoughts with partial success; automatic thoughts often center on work performance; diaphragmatic breathing assigned as homework with inconsistent follow-through.

Format:

- Opening check-in questions (4-6 open-ended, non-leading)

- Homework review section (questions to explore compliance/barriers)

- Main therapeutic activities (2-3 CBT-aligned interventions, e.g., thought challenging, behavioral experiments)

- Potential session obstacles and therapist responses

- Closing & new homework suggestions (SMART, realistic)

- Ethical/self-care reminders for therapist

Think step by step: 1) Summarize key progress themes. 2) Align to CBT principles. 3) Ensure client-centered focus. 4) Flag any over-reliance risks.

Constraints: Evidence-based only (CBT core techniques). Max 500 words. Professional, neutral tone.

End your response with this exact sentence: "This is a draft suggestion only. Review thoroughly, edit as needed, and apply your clinical judgment before use."

End your response with: "This is a draft suggestion only. Review thoroughly, edit as needed, and apply your clinical judgment before use."

Expected Output Benefits:

- Saves 10-15 minutes of manual outlining.
- Provides fresh angles (e.g., "If homework non-compliance stems from perfectionism, pivot to values clarification").
- You edit for personalization (e.g., add your rapport-building opener).

Example 2: Hypothesis Generation for Complex Cases

For clients with layered concerns (e.g., trauma + depression):

You are a reflective clinical hypothesis assistant. Draw ONLY from trauma-informed, ACT, and attachment-based frameworks. No diagnostic language.

Task: Generate 3-4 tentative hypotheses about relational or behavioral patterns based on this anonymized summary.

Context: Hypothetical long-term client: Reports recurring interpersonal withdrawal after perceived rejection; history of childhood invalidation; recent increase in avoidance behaviors.

Format:

- Hypothesis 1: [Brief description + possible maintaining factors]

- Hypothesis 2: ...

- Supporting questions to explore in session

- Suggested gentle probes (non-interpretive)

Constraints: Hypotheses are exploratory only. Emphasize curiosity over certainty. No treatment recommendations here.

Think step by step and self-check for bias.

End with the required oversight reminder.

This helps prime your curiosity without leading you to premature conclusions.

Integrating with Compliant Tools in 2026

- Twofold Health / Mentalyc: Many now offer "prep insights" or theme summaries from past notes and feed anonymized highlights into their built-in AI for agenda suggestions.
- Upheal / Eleos Health: If you use their analytics, export de-identified progress summaries to prompt for next-session focus.
- Standalone LLMs: Use ChatGPT Enterprise (BAA-enabled) or Claude for Work for pure prompt-based prep.

Workflow tip: Keep a secure "AI Prep Template" doc in your EHR or encrypted notes app. Paste anonymized summaries, run prompts, copy outputs, then delete temp files.

Common Pitfalls and Ethical Safeguards

- Pitfall: Over-relying on AI ideas - reduced creativity. Safeguard: Limit to 20-30% of your plan; always add your unique insights.
- Pitfall: Subtle bias in outputs (e.g., cultural assumptions). Safeguard: Add "Prioritize cultural humility and intersectional awareness" to prompts.
- Pitfall: Blurring lines between prep and in-session use. Safeguard: No phone/laptop open during sessions for AI reference - print or mentally note key points.
- Ethical Checkpoint: If a client asks about your prep process, disclose transparently (e.g., "I use secure, compliant tools to organize ideas, but all decisions are mine").

Case Vignette: A Solo Therapist's Weekly Routine

Dr. Maya, a private-practice counselor in Florida, sees 25 clients/week. Pre-AI: 45 minutes/client prep. Now:

- Sunday evenings: Review 5-6 upcoming files.
- Copy anonymized bullet summaries.
- Run 2-3 prompts per client (agenda + interventions).
- Spend 15 minutes editing/personalizing.

- Result: 20+ extra hours/month for self-care or extra clients.

She reports feeling more present: "AI handles the scaffolding; I bring humanity."

Pre-session AI use is low-risk, high-impact. The perfect place to build confidence before tackling documentation or other workflows. Practice with one client this week using the examples above. In the next chapters, we'll apply these skills to in-session support (with strict boundaries) and between-session tools.

Chapter 8

Documentation, Progress Notes, and Treatment Planning with AI

Documentation remains one of the heaviest burdens in mental health practice. In 2026, therapists often spend 30-50% of their professional time on progress notes, treatment plans, and related administrative tasks. This is time that could be devoted to client care, supervision, or self-care. AI, when used ethically and compliantly, can dramatically reduce this load by generating high-quality draft notes and plan elements in minutes rather than hours.

This chapter focuses on post-session documentation and treatment planning workflows. We emphasize:

- Using only HIPAA-compliant tools with signed Business Associate Agreements (BAAs).
- Starting from anonymized dictation, bullet summaries, or typed highlights (never raw audio in non-compliant systems).
- Heavy human review and editing. AI drafts are never final records.
- Common formats: DAP (Data, Assessment, Plan), SOAP (Sub-

jective, Objective, Assessment, Plan), BIRP (Behavior, Intervention, Response, Plan), and variations.

By the end, you'll have reusable workflows, prompt examples, and integration tips for leading 2026 tools.

The Current Landscape: Why AI Documentation Matters in 2026

Burnout surveys continue to rank documentation as a top contributor to clinician exhaustion. AI note-taking tools have matured significantly:

- Mentalyc - Frequently ranked #1 for psychotherapy-specific accuracy, audit-ready notes, sentiment analysis, and flexible templates (DAP, SOAP, BIRP, EMDR). No audio storage, strong privacy focus, tiered pricing (~$15-$100/month).

- Twofold Health - Often called best overall for unlimited notes, speed (<30 seconds drafts), multilingual support, and zero post-processing audio retention. Flat-rate ~$49/month; excels in private practice value.

- Upheal - Strong for session analytics, outcome tracking, and therapy-specific understanding (DAP notes prominent). Pricing ~$19-$69/month; good for insights but some plans involve recording.

- AutoNotes - Behavioral health-focused, supports structured formats from dictation/typed input. HIPAA/PHIPA compliant, subscription-based; simple for solo users.

- Supanote - Dictation-to-structured notes specialist, multiple formats (SOAP, DAP, BIRP), EHR push features; strong for unstructured input.
- Freed AI / Others - Fast drafts (15-30 seconds), but often more medicalized; check BAA for therapy fit.

Always verify current BAA, privacy policies, and clinician reviews - compliance evolves. Tools like TheraPlatform and ClinicTracker also integrate native AI with full EHR ecosystems.

Core Documentation Workflow with AI

Standard 6-step process (typically 5-15 minutes per note after initial setup):

1. Immediately Post-Session: Jot anonymized bullets or dictate key points (via compliant app) while fresh. Focus on facts, observations, client statements, interventions, responses.
2. Input to Tool/Prompt: Use built-in features or copy an anonymized summary into a prompt.
3. Generate Draft: Run AI to produce structured format.
4. Review & Edit: Check for accuracy, bias, hallucinations; add nuance; ensure objective language.
5. Finalize in EHR: Copy-paste or auto-fill; sign off.
6. Log AI Use: Note in records if required by board/malpractice.

Example 1: DAP Note Draft from Anonymized Summary

You are a HIPAA-compliant documentation assistant only. You NEVER create final clinical records, NEVER diagnose, NEVER interpret beyond provided facts, and NEVER include subjective therapist opinions unless explicitly stated.

Task: Generate a draft DAP progress note from this anonymized session summary.

Context: Hypothetical session 12. Client discussed ongoing family conflict stressors. Reported improved use of boundary-setting skills from prior homework. Affect congruent and calmer than previous. No safety concerns. Intervention: Explored cognitive distortions around guilt; practiced reframing exercise.

Format (DAP):

- Data: Bullet points of objective facts, client quotes/statements, observations

- Assessment: Neutral summary of session progress/changes (no diagnosis)

- Plan: Next steps, homework, follow-up focus

Constraints: Objective, professional language only. Max 300 words. Flag any ambiguity.

Think step by step: 1) Extract facts. 2) Organize chronologically. 3) Keep assessment descriptive. 4) Suggest realistic plan. 5) Self-check for ethical issues.

End with: "This is a draft suggestion only. Review thoroughly, edit as needed, and apply your clinical judgment before finalizing or using in records."

Typical Output (Edited Example):

- Data: Client arrived on time via telehealth. Reported "feeling less overwhelmed" after practicing boundary phrases with family. Described one successful interaction. Affect: relaxed posture, steady voice. No acute distress noted.
- Assessment: Client demonstrated progress in applying learned skills to real-life stressors; engagement remained high.
- Plan: Continue boundary work; assign journaling of one additional interaction. Next session: review journal, introduce values clarification if needed. Scheduled for [date].

Example 2: SOAP Note for Insurance/Payer Requirements

Adapt prompt for SOAP (common for billing/medical integration):

- Subjective: Client-reported symptoms/experiences.
- Objective: Observable facts.
- Assessment: Clinical impressions (neutral).
- Plan: Interventions/next steps.

Example 3: BIRP for Behavioral/Goal-Focused Therapy

BIRP suits measurable interventions:

- Behavior: Client actions/observations.
- Intervention: Therapist techniques used.
- Response: Client reaction/outcome.
- Plan: Future direction.

Prompt variation: Add "Format (BIRP): Behavior... Intervention... Resp onse... Plan..."

Treatment Planning with AI

AI shines for drafting/updating plans:

- Generate SMART goals from presenting concerns.
- Suggest objective tracking methods.
- Outline phased interventions.

Sample Prompt Snippet:

Task: Draft 3 SMART goal variations and supporting objectives for this hypothetical goal area.

Context: Hypothetical client: Building emotional regulation skills amid anger outbursts.

Format:

- Goal 1: [SMART statement]

- Measurement method

- Potential interventions (evidence-based only)

- Barriers to anticipate

Integration Tips & Pitfalls

- Tool-Specific: Mentalyc/Upheal excel at sentiment/progress tracking; Twofold for unlimited/custom templates.
- EHR Push: Tools like Supanote or TheraPlatform allow direct transfer.
- Pitfalls: Hallucinated details (fix: tight constraints); over-editing time (start simple); forgetting consent updates.
- Ethical Safeguards: Disclose AI assistance in consent forms; audit drafts; never auto-sign.

Case Vignette: From 2 Hours to 15 Minutes

A Florida-based LCSW sees 28 clients/week. Pre-AI: 45-60 min/note. Now:

- Post-session: 3-min anonymized dictation into Mentalyc.
- AI generates a DAP draft.

- 10-min review/edit.
- Copy to SimplePractice EHR.
- Savings: 15-20 hours/week - more clients, better boundaries.

Post-session documentation is where AI delivers the biggest Return on investment, particularly when paired with the prompts and principles from earlier chapters. Practice one format this week. Next, we explore in-session and between-session boundaries in Chapter 9.

Chapter 9

In-Session and Between-Session Support - Ethical Applications

The therapeutic session itself is the sacred core of mental health work: a live, embodied interaction where presence, attunement, empathy, and real-time relational repair occur. In 2026, AI has no place directly participating in this space, no live transcription during sessions (without explicit, ongoing consent and strict compliance), no real-time prompting on a screen, no AI-generated responses fed to the client. The human therapist's capacity for nuanced, moment-to-moment connection remains irreplaceable.

That said, there are limited, carefully bounded ways AI can provide

indirect, ethical support during or immediately adjacent to sessions. This chapter explores those narrow applications while reinforcing strict boundaries:

- In-session uses: Discreet, pre-prepared reference materials or quick mental prompts (no device interaction during active therapy).
- Between-session uses: Secure, non-therapeutic follow-up tools

such as homework reminders, resource sharing, or client self-guided skill reinforcement (with clear limits).

- Heavy emphasis on consent, transparency, privacy, and human oversight.

All examples assume HIPAA-compliant tools only and full adherence to the prompt engineering principles from Chapters 4-5.

In-Session Support: Indirect and Minimal

Direct in-session AI use (e.g., typing client statements into a chatbot mid-session, asking AI for real-time intervention ideas) is generally discouraged or prohibited by most ethics committees, malpractice carriers, and professional guidelines in 2026. Reasons include:

- Distraction from presence.
- Risk of PHI exposure if tools are non-compliant.
- Potential for delayed or inaccurate suggestions.
- Erosion of the therapeutic alliance if perceived as reliance on technology.

Permissible indirect approaches (low-risk, widely accepted):

1. Pre-Session Printed or Memorized Cheat Sheets Use AI-generated agendas, key questions, or intervention menus (from Chapter 7) printed or mentally rehearsed before the session. Glance at a physical page if needed during a natural pause (e.g., client journaling).

2. Silent Self-Prompting In your mind, recall a pre-crafted internal prompt structure. Example mental framework during a stuck moment: "Role: Compassionate observer. Task: Notice patterns. Constraints: No interpretation yet. Think: What core emotion might be underneath? What safety need is present?"

3. Post-Session Immediate Reflection (Immediately After Client Leaves) Jot quick anonymized bullets - run a brief "debrief prompt" (from Chapter 6 Category 6) while memory is fresh. This bridges in-session to documentation without intruding on the hour.

Ethical Guardrail: If you ever feel tempted to open a device during a session for AI input, pause and ask: "Is this enhancing presence or diluting it?" Most often, the answer is the latter.

Between-Session Support: Client-Facing Tools with Strict Boundaries

Between sessions, AI can help generate non-therapeutic, supportive materials that clients may use independently. Provided they follow the following guidelines:

- Materials are psychoeducational or skill-building only (never diagnostic, prescriptive, or simulating therapy).
- You review and personalize every piece.
- Client consent forms explicitly cover AI-assisted resource creation.

- No direct AI-to-client communication (e.g., no AI chatbot for clients).

Common applications:

1. Homework Resource Generation Create bullet-point reminders, grounding scripts, thought records templates (content only), or mindfulness exercise descriptions.

Example Prompt (copy-paste ready):

You are an ethical psychoeducation resource assistant. You do NOT provide therapy, do NOT diagnose, do NOT offer personalized advice.

Task: Generate neutral, evidence-based content for a between-session client handout.

Context: Hypothetical focus area: Building distress tolerance skills using DBT-inspired techniques.

Format:

- Brief introductory paragraph (2-4 sentences, factual)

- 4-6 specific techniques (name + 1-2 sentence how-to)

- When/how to practice

- Safety note: "Use these as general skills; contact your therapist for personalized guidance"

Constraints: Draw only from established DBT distress tolerance module. Neutral, empowering language. Max 350 words.

Think step by step. End with: "This is draft content only. Review, personalize, and obtain client consent before sharing."

Output Use: Print/email via secure portal after your edits. Client sees your name/signature, not AI.

1. Secure Portal Messages or Reminder Texts Draft brief, supportive check-ins (e.g., "Remember to practice the breathing exercise twice today if it feels helpful").

Prompt Variation:

Task: Draft 2-3 short, professional between-session encouragement messages.

Context: Hypothetical client working on sleep hygiene after anxiety management session.

Format: Short paragraphs or bullet reminders. Warm but non-therapeutic tone.

Constraints: No questions requiring response unless pre-agreed. No clinical interpretation.

1. Self-Guided Skill Reinforcement For clients using apps or journals: Provide outlines of journaling prompts or tracking sheets.

Example: "Three questions to reflect on after a triggering event: What physical sensations did you notice? What thoughts came up? What small action helped regulate?"

Consent, Transparency, and Documentation

Update your informed consent form with language such as:

"I may use HIPAA-compliant AI tools to assist in creating general psychoeducational resources, session planning outlines, or draft documentation. All materials are reviewed and personalized by me before use. AI is never used for direct therapeutic interaction, diagnosis, or treatment decisions."

Document in notes when AI-assisted materials are provided (e.g., "Provided client with AI-reviewed grounding handout on [date]; client verbalized understanding").

Pitfalls and Safeguards

- Pitfall: Clients becoming overly reliant on handouts - reduced self-efficacy. Safeguard: Frame resources as "optional tools to complement our work together."
- Pitfall: Perceived "dehumanization" if the client learns about AI. Safeguard: Normalize: "Like using a calculator for math, AI helps with organization so I can be more present."
- Pitfall: Blurring lines into therapy-by-proxy. Safeguard: Never promise AI will "help" in crisis; always direct to emergency contacts.

Case Vignette: Balanced Integration

Maria, a trauma-focused therapist in California, uses AI between sessions only for resource creation. After teaching grounding, she runs a prompt for a customized (but general) 5-4-3-2-1 script variation. She edits, prints it with her letterhead, and discusses it in the next session. Client reports: "It's helpful to have something tangible, but I still need our talks to process." Maria feels more efficient without compromising depth.

In-session and between-session AI must remain peripheral - supportive scaffolding, never the main structure. The next chapter covers client-facing tools and homework boundaries in greater detail.

Chapter 10

Client-Facing Tools - Handouts, Resources, and Homework (with Boundaries)

One of the most appreciated ways therapists use AI is to create high-quality, tailored psychoeducational materials and homework supports quickly, saving hours that would otherwise be spent researching, writing, and formatting handouts from scratch. In 2026, AI excels at generating clear, evidence-based content in seconds, but these outputs must remain strictly non-therapeutic, general, reviewable, and non-directive to stay within ethical and legal boundaries.

This chapter covers the safe, compliant creation of client-facing tools: psychoeducation handouts, skill-building guides, journaling prompts, tracking sheets (content ideas only), and between-session reinforcement materials. We focus on:

- Strict boundaries to prevent AI from crossing into therapy-by-proxy.
- Consent and transparency requirements.

- Prompt templates that enforce safety.
- Real-world examples and customization tips.
- When not to use AI for client materials.

Core Boundaries for Client-Facing AI Use

Client-facing materials generated with AI must never:

- Diagnose, interpret symptoms, or offer personalized treatment recommendations.
- Simulate therapeutic dialogue, empathy, or relational repair.
- Provide crisis intervention, safety planning, or suicide/self-harm guidance (always direct to live human support).
- Replace your clinical judgment or the therapeutic alliance.
- Be delivered without your full review, personalization, and signature/branding.

Always frame materials as general resources to complement - not substitute - your work together.

Required safeguards:

- Update informed consent: "I may use secure, HIPAA-compliant AI tools to assist in creating general psychoeducational handouts or skill-building outlines. All materials are reviewed, edited, and approved by me before sharing."

- Document provision: Note in the record (e.g., "Provided client with reviewed grounding techniques handout on [date]; client verbalized understanding and intent to use as needed").
- Client acknowledgment: Verbal or written confirmation that materials are optional and general.

Workflow for Creating Client-Facing Materials

Standard 5-step process (typically 5-12 minutes per handout):

1. Identify Need - During or after a session, note a skill or concept the client could benefit from reviewing (e.g., grounding, cognitive distortions, boundary-setting).
2. Anonymize & Prompt - Use a safe, constrained prompt with hypothetical context.
3. Generate Draft - Run in compliant tool (Mentalyc, Twofold Health, or BAA-enabled LLM).
4. Review & Personalize - Edit tone, add your insights, remove anything directive, format for readability (bullet points, simple language).
5. Deliver Securely - Via encrypted portal, email with encryption, or printed handout with your letterhead. Never via unsecured text or client-chosen AI apps.

Example 1: Psychoeducation Handout on Grounding Techniques

You are an ethical psychoeducation content assistant. You do NOT provide therapy, do NOT diagnose, do NOT offer personalized advice or treatment plans.

Task: Create a concise, neutral handout on grounding techniques for managing intense emotions or dissociation.

Context: General audience - adults seeking basic self-regulation skills. No specific client details.

Format:

- Title: Grounding Techniques for Managing Intense Moments

- Introduction (2-4 sentences, factual purpose)

- 5-7 specific techniques (name + 1-2 sentence description + when to use)

- General tips for practice

- Important safety note: "These are general skills only. Contact your therapist or a crisis line if you are in distress or unsafe."

Constraints: Draw only from evidence-based mindfulness and sensory-based approaches recognized by APA/ACA. Neutral, empowering, non-directive language. Max 450 words. Use simple, accessible wording (8th-grade reading level).

Think step by step: 1) List established techniques. 2) Ensure factual accuracy. 3) Avoid any therapeutic framing. 4) Self-check for over-prescription.

End with: "This is draft content only. Review thoroughly, personalize for your client, and obtain consent before sharing."

After Your Edits - Add your practice logo, a footer ("Prepared by [Your Name], LMHC - For educational use only"), and one sentence tying it to session work (e.g., "We discussed the 5-4-3-2-1 technique in our last session - here's a reminder sheet").

Example 2: Thought Record Outline (CBT-Inspired)

Task: Generate a simple thought record template outline (content only - no instructions on how to use therapeutically).

Context: General cognitive restructuring support for adults.

Format:

- Column headers with brief description of what to write in each

- 1-2 example rows (hypothetical, neutral situations)

- Footer safety note

Constraints: CBT-based structure only (Situation, Automatic Thought, Evidence For/Against, Balanced Thought, Outcome). No interpretive guidance. Max 300 words.

Your Role: Convert to a clean PDF or printable sheet; add your own brief intro: "Use this format if it feels helpful between sessions - we can review together next time."

Example 3: Journaling Prompts for Values Clarification (ACT-Inspired)

Task: Provide 6-8 open-ended journaling prompts focused on personal values exploration.

Context: General adult audience.

Format: Numbered list of prompts only.

Constraints: Draw from ACT values clarification principles. Keep neutral and non-directive - no analysis or follow-up questions. No therapeutic framing.

When NOT to Use AI for Client Materials

- Crisis or high-risk situations (suicidality, abuse, acute decompensation).
- Clients with paranoia, tech mistrust, or strong preference for "human-only" materials.
- Any content requiring deep cultural nuance you haven't vetted.
- Materials intended for legal/forensic use (court-mandated reports, custody evaluations).

Case Vignette: From Generic PDFs to Personalized Tools

Dr. Raj, a Miami-based psychologist, previously relied on stock worksheets from therapy sites. Now:

- After teaching progressive muscle relaxation, he runs a prompt for a customized 8-step script variation.
- Edits for client's reading level and cultural references (e.g., incorporates beach imagery for Florida clients).
- Emails secure PDF via Spruce Health portal.
- Client feedback: "Having it in my own words from you makes it feel more real."

Result: Higher homework compliance, stronger alliance, less prep time.

Client-facing tools are a powerful extension of your work when kept firmly in the "educational support" lane. They amplify your voice without replacing it. In the next chapters, we compare tools head-to-head, outline full practice implementation, and look toward future trends.

detail, followed by tool comparisons and full implementation in Chapters 11-12.

Chapter 11

Comparing AI Tools for Therapists in 2026 - General vs. Specialized

By March 2026, the AI tool landscape for mental health professionals has matured into two clear and distinct categories: general-purpose compliant large language models, such as ChatGPT Enterprise and Claude for Work, and specialized behavioral health platforms purpose-built for therapy notes, clinical workflows, and compliance. Choosing between them or combining them strategically, is one of the most consequential decisions a therapist can make when integrating AI into their practice.

This chapter compares the leading options head-to-head, focusing on what matters most for working clinicians: HIPAA compliance and BAA availability, privacy practices including audio retention and data training policies, clinical accuracy for psychotherapy-specific language, note format support across DAP, SOAP, BIRP, and variations, pricing and scalability, and the real-world drawbacks that don't always appear in marketing materials.

The goal is not to sell you on any single tool. It is to give you a framework for evaluating the rapidly evolving landscape so you can make decisions that protect your clients, your license, and your time.

Why the Tool You Choose Matters More Than You Think

Many therapists approach AI tool selection the way they might choose a scheduling app - with a rough sense that "most of them do roughly the same thing." This assumption is costly. The differences between tools are not cosmetic. A platform without a signed BAA puts every session note you generate through it at potential HIPAA risk. A tool that retains audio post-processing could expose client conversations to data breaches or model training pipelines. A system that generates verbose, inaccurate drafts may actually cost you more time to edit than it saves.

On the other hand, the right tool, matched to your caseload, modality, and workflow can reclaim eight to fifteen hours per week, reduce documentation-related burnout by measurable margins, and let you show up more fully in session. The choice matters.

Key Evaluation Criteria

When assessing any AI tool for therapy practice, evaluate it across these dimensions:

Compliance and Privacy. Does the tool offer a signed Business Associate Agreement? Does it retain audio after processing? Does it train its models on your data? Is it SOC 2 or HITRUST certified? These are non-negotiables, not nice-to-haves.

Therapy-Specific Accuracy. Can the tool handle the nuanced language of psychotherapy - distinguishing affect from mood, capturing relational dynamics, using appropriate clinical terminology without over-diagnosing? General models often miss this. Specialized tools are trained on it.

Speed and Usability. How long does a draft take to generate? How much editing is typically required? Is the interface intuitive enough that you will actually use it consistently under the pressure of a full caseload?

Note Format Support. Does the tool support your preferred formats? DAP, SOAP, BIRP, GIRP, EMDR-specific notes? Can you customize templates for your theoretical orientation?

Pricing and Scalability. Is the pricing model flat-rate or tiered by volume? Does it penalize you as your caseload grows? Is it viable for solo practice, or is it designed for enterprise settings?

Honest Drawbacks. Every tool has limitations. A tool whose marketing materials don't acknowledge any weaknesses is a tool whose weaknesses haven't been found yet, or aren't being disclosed.

Specialized Behavioral Health Platforms

Twofold Health consistently ranks at or near the top in 2026 clinician surveys for private and group practice use. Its defining features are zero post-processing audio retention, unlimited note generation at a flat monthly rate of approximately $49, and a privacy architecture that separates psychotherapy notes from general session content per HIPAA's heightened protections. Draft generation takes roughly thirty seconds. Templates support DAP, SOAP, BIRP, and custom formats. The primary limitation is that Twofold's analytics capabilities are less developed than competitors focused on session insights. It is optimized for documentation speed and privacy, not trend tracking.

Mentalyc leads the field in psychotherapy-specific clinical accuracy. Its sentiment analysis engine, progress-tracking features, and Alliance Genie tool (which flags potential therapeutic alliance ruptures based on session content), make it the preferred choice for insight-driven clinicians. Notes are accurate and typically require fewer edits than competitors. Pricing is tiered from approximately $19 to $100 per month based on volume. The main drawback is that drafts can occasionally run verbose, requiring more trimming than some clinicians prefer, and the platform is primarily browser-based with a learning curve for complex template customization.

Upheal differentiates itself through session analytics and outcome tracking, features that go beyond note generation to help clinicians understand patterns across their caseload. Its DAP notes are strong, and its telehealth integration is seamless. Pricing ranges from approximately $19 to $69 per month. The tradeoff is that some Upheal plans involve session recording, which requires explicit client consent and careful disclosure management. The interface can feel complex for clinicians who want simplicity over depth.

AutoNotes serves therapists who prioritize speed and simplicity above all else. It is HIPAA and PHIPA compliant, supports structured SOAP, DAP, and BIRP formats, and generates drafts from dictated or typed input in roughly one minute. Pricing is subscription-based and accessible for solo practitioners. The limitations are real: less customization depth than Mentalyc or Twofold, fewer integrations, and a smaller clinical community providing reviews and peer validation.

Supanote and Freed AI round out the specialized tier. Supanote excels at EHR push functionality and deep customization for practitioners already embedded in specific electronic health record systems. Freed AI generates drafts quickly, often in thirty to forty-five seconds, and supports over thirty templates, though its orientation is broader than purely behavioral health and drafts may require more clinical editing for psychotherapy-specific language.

General-Purpose Compliant LLMs

ChatGPT Enterprise and Claude for Work occupy a different category. They are not purpose-built for therapy, but in the hands of a clinician who has mastered the prompt engineering principles in Chapters 4 and 5, they become extraordinarily capable tools for brainstorming, resource creation, session planning, and complex reasoning tasks.

The critical requirement is enterprise-level access. Free and standard consumer tiers of ChatGPT and Claude do not include Business Associate Agreements and should never be used with client information of any kind. Enterprise accounts unlock BAA availability, data isolation, and training data opt-out provisions that make compliant use possible.

The advantages of general LLMs are flexibility and reasoning depth. Claude, for instance, excels at sustained, multi-step reasoning and long-context tasks, making it well-suited for complex treatment planning, case conceptualization, or generating nuanced psychoeducational content. ChatGPT Enterprise offers broad template support and strong structured output generation. Gemini for Workspace integrates naturally with Google's productivity suite, a useful feature for clinicians already working within that ecosystem.

The disadvantages are equally clear. Without therapy-specific training, these models have higher hallucination rates on clinical language, less accurate understanding of therapeutic modality distinctions, and no native note templates. They require more refined prompting to produce consistent, usable outputs.

The Hybrid Approach: What Most Successful Clinicians Actually Do

The most experienced AI-using therapists in 2026 don't pick one tool and commit exclusively. They layer. A typical high-performing workflow looks like this: a specialized platform like Twofold or Mentalyc handles all post-session documentation, the high-volume, time-sensitive work where accuracy and speed matter most. A compliant general LLM handles brainstorming, resource generation, complex case conceptualization, and tasks that benefit from deeper, more flexible reasoning. The two tools serve different purposes and rarely overlap.

This approach costs slightly more per month than a single-tool solution, but the time savings and quality improvements justify the investment for most full-caseload practices.

Quick Decision Guide

If you are a solo or small practice on a budget who wants maximum privacy and unlimited notes, Twofold Health is the strongest choice. If clinical insight and psychotherapy-specific accuracy matter most, Mentalyc leads. If you want session analytics and outcome tracking alongside strong notes, consider Upheal. If you are already in an enterprise EHR ecosystem, investigate whether your platform has native AI integration before subscribing to anything else. If you have mastered prompt engineering and want maximum flexibility, a compliant general LLM paired with a specialized note tool gives you the deepest capability.

Whatever you choose, verify the current BAA status and privacy policy directly with the vendor before entering any client information. This landscape evolves quickly. What is true in March 2026 may shift by the time you read this.

Chapter 12

Step-by-Step Implementation - From First Use to Full Integration

The gap between knowing AI can help your practice and actually experiencing that help is not a gap of information. Most therapists considering AI adoption in 2026 have read articles, watched webinars, and talked to colleagues who rave about reclaiming their evenings. The gap is implementation, the practical, week-by-week process of going from "I should try this" to "I cannot imagine practicing without it."

This chapter provides that process. Not as a theoretical framework, but as a realistic, sequenced twelve-week plan grounded in how actual clinicians have successfully integrated AI into working practices. It accounts for the resistance you will feel, the learning curve you will navigate, and the moments where the technology will frustrate you before it transforms you.

Twelve weeks is not an arbitrary timeline. It reflects the research on habit formation and workflow change in professional settings. Sustainable integration requires enough time to move through experimentation, stumbling, refinement, and genuine adoption, without rushing past the stages that build real confidence and safety.

Before You Begin: The Preparation Mindset

The clinicians who integrate AI most successfully share a common orientation before they ever open a tool. They approach the process the way they approach a new therapeutic modality, with structured curiosity, a willingness to be a beginner, and a commitment to tracking what works and what doesn't.

They also begin with clarity about their primary pain point. Is it documentation? Session planning? Resource creation? The clinicians who try to do everything at once typically do nothing well. The ones who start with a single, specific problem and solve it completely before expanding are the ones who reach full integration.

Before beginning the twelve-week plan, spend thirty minutes on one honest assessment: in a typical week, where does administrative burden hurt most? That answer tells you where to start.

Phase 1: Preparation (Weeks 1-2)

Self-assessment and pain point mapping. Track your time for one full week. Note how long documentation actually takes, not how long you think it takes. Most therapists are genuinely surprised. The average clinician underestimates documentation time by thirty to forty percent.

Compliance foundation. Review the APA's 2025 Ethical Guidance for AI in the Professional Practice of Health Service Psychology. Update your informed consent forms with a clear AI disclosure statement before you use any tool with client-adjacent information. Consult your malpractice carrier, most approve note drafting with human oversight, but verify for your specific coverage and jurisdiction. Do not skip this step. Compliance infrastructure before clinical use is not bureaucracy. It is protection for you and your clients.

Tool selection and trial. Choose one tool only. Not two, not three. Based on the criteria in Chapter 11, select the platform most aligned with your workflow and begin its free trial. Sign the BAA before proceeding. Create a secure folder in your EHR or encrypted drive labeled "AI Drafts". This is a home for outputs awaiting your review and editing.

Anonymization practice. Before entering anything, practice anonymizing session content. Remove all eighteen HIPAA identifiers. If you are not yet fluent in this, practice with fictional scenarios until the habit is automatic.

Phase 2: Safe Experimentation (Weeks 3-6)

This is the phase where most therapists either build momentum or abandon the process. The key is radical constraint; doing far less than feels necessary, and doing it consistently.

Week 3 - Pre-session work only. Use AI exclusively for session planning. Run three to five agenda prompts using the templates from Chapter 7 on hypothetical or fully anonymized past cases. Do not attempt documentation yet. Simply learn how the tool responds to your prompts, how much editing the outputs need, and how to refine your inputs for better results.

Week 4 - Post-session documentation begins. After sessions, spend three minutes dictating anonymized bullets into your tool; key observations, interventions, responses, next steps. Generate a DAP draft. Edit it completely, as if you had written it from scratch and were proofreading for accuracy. Time yourself. Compare that time to your previous documentation method. The data you collect this week will sustain your motivation through the harder weeks ahead.

Week 5 - Resource and handout creation. Use the prompts from Chapter 10 to generate one to two psychoeducational handouts or homework supports. Edit them, personalize them with your voice and your client's needs, and deliver them through your secure portal or as printed materials. Notice how clients respond to receiving more consistent, polished between-session support.

Week 6 - Between-session communications. Draft brief, professional check-in messages or session reminders for consenting clients using the prompts from Chapter 9. Keep them non-therapeutic, they should be informational and supportive only.

Throughout Phase 2, maintain a simple log: for each AI-assisted task, note the time it took, how much editing was required, and whether the output was usable. This data is your compass.

Phase 3: Building Durable Habits (Weeks 7-10)

By week seven, most clinicians have identified two to three AI workflows that consistently save time and produce quality outputs. Phase 3 is about systemizing those workflows so they become automatic rather than deliberate.

Documentation routine. Aim for eighty percent of your progress notes to move through AI drafting. Your target is under fifteen minutes per note, including dictation, generation, editing, and finalizing in your EHR. If you are not hitting that mark, revisit your prompts using the principles in Chapter 5; tighter constraints, more explicit format instructions, clearer context.

Prompt refinement library. Save your best-performing prompts as templates in a document or directly within your tool. Note which prompts produce outputs that need the least editing. Annotate them with what makes them effective. This prompt library is one of the most valuable professional assets you will build.

Client disclosure conversations. Have an explicit conversation about AI with five to ten clients. You might say something like: "I want to be transparent, I use secure, HIPAA-compliant AI tools to help organize my notes and sometimes to generate educational handouts. Everything is reviewed and edited by me before it becomes part of your record or anything I share with you. Do you have any questions or concerns about that?" Most clients respond with curiosity or relief, relief that you are using available tools to be more present with them, not more burdened by paperwork.

Metric tracking. By week ten, you should have enough data to answer these questions: How many hours per week am I saving? What percentage of AI outputs require significant editing versus light editing? How has my experience of the workday changed? These answers are not just motivational, they are the foundation for responsible, evidence-informed continued use.

Phase 4: Full Integration and Long-Term Sustainability (Weeks 11-12 and Beyond)

Full integration does not mean AI handles everything. It means AI handles what it does well, reliably, safely, and efficiently, while you bring full human presence to what only you can do.

Complete documentation workflow. Ninety to one hundred percent of documentation moves through AI drafting. Treatment plans, progress notes, and session planning materials are generated as drafts and refined by your clinical judgment. The time you save is deliberately protected, it does not simply fill with other administrative tasks.

Monthly quality audits. Review five notes per month for accuracy, clinical appropriateness, and potential bias. Look specifically for over-generalization, hallucinated details, or language that doesn't reflect your actual clinical impressions. Adjust your prompts when you find patterns.

Ongoing education. Subscribe to APA Monitor on Psychology's AI coverage. Follow your tool's changelog and update communications. Revisit the tool comparison landscape every six months. This field moves quickly, and the best option in 2026 may not be the best option in 2027.

Series expansion. If you are using AI for one category of tasks and not others, consider whether there are additional workflows that could benefit. The clinicians who report the highest satisfaction with AI integration are those who have systematically evaluated every time-consuming administrative task against the question: could a well-engineered prompt and a compliant tool handle the drafting of this, with my oversight?

Common Roadblocks and How to Move Through Them

Hallucinations and inaccurate outputs. If your tool is frequently generating content that doesn't match your session, the problem is almost always prompt quality. Return to Chapter 5 and tighten your constraints, specify your context more precisely, and add explicit step-by-step reasoning instructions.

Resistance from within. Some therapists feel genuine discomfort using AI for clinical-adjacent work. Sometimes they harbor a sense that it is somehow less authentic or caring. This deserves honest examination. If your clients are receiving better-quality notes, more consistent resources, and a more present therapist because documentation is less exhausting, the care they receive has increased, not decreased. The discomfort is often about identity, what it means to be a good clinician, not about the actual impact on clients.

Technology overwhelms. If you feel overwhelmed, you are almost certainly trying to do too much at once. Return to one tool, one workflow, one week at a time. The twelve-week plan is structured specifically to prevent overwhelm, but only if you follow its pacing.

Chapter 13

Case Studies - Real-World Wins, Pitfalls, and Lessons Learned

The distance between reading about AI integration and actually integrating it can feel enormous. Statistics and frameworks, however well-constructed, don't fully capture what it is like to sit at your desk after a full day of sessions, open a tool for the first time, type an anonymized summary into a prompt, and watch a draft note appear in thirty seconds that would have taken you forty-five minutes to write.

The following case studies are drawn from composite experiences of licensed mental health professionals who have navigated this transition in 2025 and 2026. Names and identifying details have been changed. Their stories are included not to present AI adoption as universally smooth or uncomplicated, but to illustrate the reality, the friction, the turning points, and the moments of genuine relief. Their stories are included so that you can recognize your own experience in theirs and keep moving forward when it gets hard.

Case Study 1: The Solo Practitioner Who Got Her Evenings Back

Sarah is a licensed mental health counselor in private practice in central Florida. She maintains a caseload of twenty-eight clients per week, specializing in anxiety and trauma. Before integrating AI, her evenings looked like this: dinner with her family, then two to three hours at her desk completing notes before bed. She had been doing this for eleven years. She had accepted it as the cost of private practice.

In early 2026, a colleague mentioned Twofold Health at a peer consultation group. Sarah was skeptical, she had read about AI hallucinations, worried about HIPAA, and frankly wasn't sure she trusted a technology she didn't fully understand to be involved in her clinical record.

She decided to try it for two weeks before making any judgment. She started with her most straightforward cases. Adult clients with relatively uncomplicated presentations where the notes followed a predictable structure. After each session, she dictated a three-minute anonymized summary (presenting topic, intervention used, client response, plan), and let the tool generate a DAP draft.

The first draft she read surprised her. It was not perfect, but it was not bad either. It captured the structure she would have used, organized her observations in a logical sequence, and gave her something to edit rather than something to create from scratch. Editing took her seven minutes instead of forty-five. She checked the clock twice because she didn't believe it.

By the end of week two, she was using the tool for all twenty-eight clients. By week six, she had reduced her evening documentation time from two to three hours to thirty to forty minutes, most of which was the editing and EHR transfer she had always done, not the writing. Her evenings returned. She started leaving her desk before her children went to bed.

The lesson Sarah emphasizes when she tells this story is not about the technology, it is about the editing mindset. "I never accepted a draft as final," she says. "Every note went through me before it went into the record. That didn't feel like extra work, it felt like what I was always supposed to be doing, but now the scaffolding was already there."

Case Study 2: The Group Practice That Caught Alliance Ruptures Early

A community mental health clinic in Northern California with six therapists began piloting Mentalyc in mid-2025, primarily as a documentation solution. What they discovered over the following months was something they hadn't anticipated. The platform's sentiment analysis and Alliance Genie features were surfacing patterns they had been missing.

Two months into the pilot, the system flagged an elevated rupture-risk score for a client being seen by one of the clinic's early-career therapists. The therapist reviewed the session transcript, discussed it in supervision, and in the next session deliberately addressed the therapeutic relationship directly. The client disclosed that she had been feeling unheard for several weeks but hadn't known how to bring it up. The rupture was repaired. The client remained in treatment.

Without the AI-assisted pattern recognition, this rupture might have resulted in a dropout, one of the most common and least-discussed outcomes in community mental health. The clinic tracked their dropout rates before and after the Mentalyc implementation and found a fifteen percent reduction over twelve months.

The pitfall they encountered was in the first six weeks: draft notes were frequently verbose and required significant editing to meet the clinical brevity standard expected by their EHR and billing team. The solution was custom template calibration. The staff worked with Mentalyc's support team to adjust output length constraints and modality-specific language expectations. After that adjustment, editing time dropped to an average of nine minutes per note.

The lesson from this case is about looking beyond the obvious. The group practice adopted AI for documentation efficiency and discovered a clinical quality improvement capability they hadn't known to ask for.

Case Study 3: The Pitfall of Over-Reliance

Marcus is a licensed psychologist in private practice in the Midwest with fifteen years of experience. He was an early adopter of AI documentation tools, and by late 2025 he had become, by his own description, "dangerously comfortable" with AI-generated outputs.

The incident that changed his practice happened on a Tuesday afternoon. He had seen seven clients back-to-back, was running on coffee and fatigue, and accepted an AI-generated assessment section in a progress note without reading it carefully. The note described a client as "demonstrating increased emotional regulation and reduced symptom severity". It was an accurate summary of the previous session, not the session he had just completed, in which the client had disclosed a significant relapse.

He caught the error during his end-of-day review, corrected the note, and documented the actual session accurately. No harm came to the client. But the near-miss shook him.

He implemented what he now calls a two-pass review rule: every AI-generated draft is read once for content accuracy (does it reflect what actually happened?), and once for clinical appropriateness (does the language reflect his professional judgment about the client's status?) The extra two minutes per note has never felt burdensome since.

The lesson Marcus shares is both simple and important: AI fatigue is real. The same cognitive shortcuts that lead experienced clinicians to miss things in complex cases can lead them to accept AI outputs too readily, especially under high-volume conditions. The oversight requirement in every prompt template in this book is not legal boilerplate. It is a genuine clinical safeguard.

Case Study 4: The Hybrid Approach in Action

Dr. Priya is a trauma-focused therapist in Austin, Texas, who sees primarily EMDR and somatic therapy clients. She describes her AI integration as "layered", a word that captures her approach well.

For documentation, she uses Twofold Health - fast, private, flat-rate, and accurate enough that her average editing time is under ten minutes per EMDR session note. For session planning and resource creation, she uses Claude for Work under her enterprise BAA. She has built a prompt library of forty-seven templates tailored specifically to trauma-informed care. Agenda outlines that sequence EMDR phases appropriately, psychoeducation handouts on the window of tolerance written at different reading levels for different clients, and between-session skill reinforcement guides in both English and Spanish.

The combination took her approximately three months to build and refine. She estimates it saves her twelve hours per week. Those hours go to her own trauma therapy, weekly supervision, and evening walks she describes as "non-negotiable since I started getting them back."

Her framing of the technology is worth sitting with: "I don't think of AI as doing my job. I think of it as handling the filing so I can actually do my job. The therapy still happens in the room, between two humans. Everything else is administration."

Lessons Across the Cases

Several themes emerge consistently across these and similar stories from 2025 and 2026:

Time savings are real but must be protected. Every clinician in these cases initially worried that reclaimed time would simply be absorbed by other administrative tasks. The ones who successfully protected it were intentional, they made an explicit commitment about what the saved time would be used for before they began.

Oversight is not optional. The Marcus case illustrates what happens when oversight becomes perfunctory. The purpose of the human-in-the-loop requirement is not compliance theater, it is clinical accuracy. Every output requires genuine engagement, not a tired skim.

The learning curve is front-loaded. Every clinician in these cases experienced the most friction in the first three to six weeks. Every one of them describes week seven or eight as a turning point, the moment when the workflows became automatic and the time savings became real. Persistence through the early discomfort is the single most important predictor of successful integration.

Clients respond better than expected. In every case where clients were informed about AI-assisted documentation and resource creation, the response was neutral to positive. No client in any of these cases requested that AI not be used in their care after a transparent explanation.

Chapter 14

Burnout Reduction, Self-Care, and Long-Term Sustainability

There is a particular exhaustion that belongs to therapists alone, the kind that comes not from physical labor but from the sustained act of holding space for other people's pain. You sit in it all day: grief, trauma, relational rupture, crisis. You witness it with full presence. You regulate your own nervous system while simultaneously attuning to another person's. You do this eight, ten, twelve times in a single day. Then you go home and write it all down.

The burnout literature in mental health is extensive and sobering. The statistics are cited throughout this book; seventy-seven percent of therapists experience significant mental fatigue. Documentation consumes thirty-five percent of working hours, charting is ranked as the leading driver of burnout. These are not just numbers. They are the texture of a professional crisis that has been building for years and reached a kind of critical mass in the mid-2020s.

AI integration, when implemented with the care and structure this book has described, addresses one part of that crisis directly: it removes the administrative weight that steals hours from the work therapists love. But removing a burden is not the same as building sustainability. This chapter is about both, the specific ways AI can reduce burnout risk, and the broader habits and structures that allow therapists to practice for the long term without losing themselves in the process.

What AI Can Actually Do for Burnout

The most direct pathway from AI integration to burnout reduction is time. When documentation consistently takes seven to twelve minutes instead of forty-five, and when that change holds across twenty-five or thirty clients per week, the math is compelling: eight to fifteen hours per week returned to the clinician. Over a month, that is thirty to sixty hours. Over a year, it approaches what some therapists describe as "getting a part-time life back."

But the research on burnout suggests that time alone is not sufficient. Clinicians who reclaim time but fill it immediately with more clients, more administrative obligations, or more anxiety about their practice don't report meaningful reductions in burnout. The time savings matter only when they are consciously redirected toward what replenishes rather than depletes.

There is a second, subtler pathway from AI to burnout reduction that gets less attention: cognitive load. Documentation requires sustained cognitive engagement: holding the session in memory, translating clinical observations into structured language, maintaining accuracy across multiple client presentations. When this cognitive labor extends into evenings and weekends, it prevents the neurological recovery that rest is supposed to provide. The brain stays in "work mode" even when the body is home. AI drafting reduces the cognitive demand of documentation significantly.

The therapist still reviews and edits, still engages clinically with the output, but the exhausting act of generating structure from a blank page is largely removed.

A third pathway is what might be called the presence dividend. Therapists who are not dreading their documentation backlog during sessions report being more present with clients. They are less likely to be mentally composing the note while the client is speaking. They arrive at each session with less anticipatory fatigue. This is not a soft benefit, it is a direct clinical quality improvement, and therapists who experience it consistently describe it as one of the most meaningful changes in their professional lives.

Using AI for Therapist Self-Care

The tools and prompts in this book have been framed primarily around client-facing workflows: notes, plans, resources. But AI can also support the therapist's own reflective and self-care practices in ways that are both practical and genuinely restorative.

Post-session debrief prompts. After a particularly difficult session, one involving acute crisis, trauma disclosure, or intense countertransference, a structured debrief prompt can help you process and discharge what you've just held. The goal is not to analyze the client but to create space for your own professional and emotional experience. A prompt might look like this:

"You are a reflective supervision assistant for licensed therapists. Your role is to help me process a professionally challenging session. Do not analyze the client or offer clinical interpretations. Focus entirely on my experience as the clinician.

Context: I just completed a session that involved [brief description of the clinical challenge - no client identifiers]. I noticed [physical or emotional reactions during session].

Please offer: 1) Grounding questions I can sit with, 2) Prompts for exploring my countertransference without judgment, 3) Self-care suggestions appropriate to this type of session content, 4) A reminder of when peer consultation or personal supervision might be warranted.

End with: 'This reflection is for your personal use only. It is not clinical documentation.'"

This kind of structured self-reflection takes five to ten minutes. It is not a replacement for supervision, personal therapy, or peer consultation, all of which remain essential. But it is an accessible, available tool for processing the immediate aftermath of the sessions that cost the most.

Supervision preparation prompts. Before a peer consultation or supervision session, AI can help you structure your thinking by organizing what you want to present, identifying the specific questions you want to explore, and surfacing patterns you might not have noticed at the moment.

Boundary-setting scripts. For therapists who struggle with professional boundary-settings; the calls that come in after hours, the clients who resist session endings, the colleagues who encroach on protected time. AI can help draft the kind of direct, compassionate communication that many helping professionals find genuinely difficult to produce under stress.

Burnout self-assessment prompts. Periodically prompting AI to generate a structured self-assessment, drawing on validated instruments like the Maslach Burnout Inventory's conceptual framework, can help therapists notice early warning signs before they become crises. The prompt should be explicit that this is personal reflection, not clinical documentation.

Sustainable Habits for the Long Haul

AI is one tool in a broader sustainability ecosystem. The therapists who maintain long, healthy, fulfilling careers share habits that no technology can replicate.

Protect the time you save. This deserves its own named commitment. Before you implement any AI workflow, decide explicitly what the reclaimed time will be used for. Write it down. Tell a colleague. The default is for reclaimed time to fill immediately with other obligations. This is exactly how people who save fifteen hours per week still report no change in their experience of their workday. Deliberate protection of reclaimed time is an act of professional self-respect.

Maintain supervision and peer consultation. No amount of AI-assisted reflection replaces the experience of being genuinely witnessed by a colleague or supervisor who knows your work. These relationships are not bureaucratic requirements. They are the professional infrastructure that sustains clinical judgment, catches blind spots, and reminds you why the work matters.

Monitor yourself with the same rigor you apply to clients. Therapists are trained observers of other people's emotional states and behavioral patterns. Applying that same observational skill to yourself, noticing the early signs of compassion fatigue, emotional numbing, or boundary erosion, is a professional competency, not a luxury.

Consider personal therapy. The research is consistent: therapists who are in or have recently been in their own therapy show lower burnout rates, stronger therapeutic alliances, and better clinical outcomes. If your own therapy has lapsed, the hours AI returns to you may be the most important investment you can make, in yourself and in your clients.

Build what one therapist calls an AI-free hour. A daily period of genuine cognitive rest, no notes, no prompts, no tools, no optimization, is part of the recovery cycle that sustained clinical practice requires. The goal of AI integration is not to produce more. It is to produce better, with less cost to the person doing the producing.

A Note on the Deeper Question

There is a version of burnout prevention that addresses symptoms: documentation burden, time pressure, and administrative load, and there is a version that addresses roots. The roots of clinician burnout are complex: systemic underfunding of mental health services, inadequate parity enforcement, the structural isolation of private practice, the weight of bearing witness to collective trauma at scale.

AI cannot fix these things. This book does not pretend it can. What AI can do is give you your evenings back, reduce the administrative friction that erodes the joy of clinical work, and free some portion of your cognitive and emotional capacity for what restores you. That is meaningful. It is not everything, but it is real, and it is available to you now.

The therapists who thrive in this profession for decades do so because they have found a way to sustain the self that does the work. AI, at its best, serves that project.

Chapter 15

The Future of AI in Psychotherapy - Trends, Predictions, and Staying Ahead

In early 2026, we are somewhere between the beginning and the middle of a transformation that will shape mental health practice for a generation. The tools available today which can generate a clinical note in thirty seconds, create a tailored psychoeducational handout in five minutes, and surface potential alliance ruptures in a session transcript, would have seemed extraordinary five years ago. In five more years, they will likely seem rudimentary.

This chapter looks forward. Not with the breathless optimism of technology marketing, nor with the reflexive skepticism that has sometimes slowed the adoption of genuinely beneficial innovations in healthcare. Rather, with the same careful, evidence-informed, ethics-first orientation that has guided everything in this book.

The future of AI in psychotherapy is not a single destination. It is a terrain that clinicians will need to navigate continuously, adapting as tools evolve, as guidelines are updated, as research accumulates, and as the meaning of "good clinical practice" expands to incorporate new capabilities and new responsibilities.

What Is Coming: Five Trends Worth Watching

Agentic and multi-agent AI systems. The AI tools of 2025-2026 largely operate in single-session, single-task mode; you provide a prompt, you receive an output, you review and act. The emerging generation of agentic AI operates differently. These systems can be given a goal; "prepare this week's session documentation and planning materials", and complete it across multiple steps, coordinating between different tools and data sources without requiring human input at each stage.

For therapists, this means AI workflows that could move from post-session dictation, through note generation, to treatment plan updating, to between-session resource preparation, with minimal manual orchestration. The efficiency gains are potentially significant. The oversight requirements become more complex and more important. When an AI agent is completing multiple linked tasks, the human review must be applied at the output level, not just the step level.

The ethical imperative is unchanged: every decision that affects a client's care requires clinician review and authorization. The form of that review will evolve as the capabilities evolve.

Predictive analytics and early warning systems. The session analytics tools available in 2026: sentiment tracking, alliance monitoring, engagement pattern analysis, are early versions of what predictive analytics will become. Within the next several years, AI systems trained on large, appropriately consented clinical datasets will likely be capable of identifying elevated dropout risk, early indicators of clinical deterioration, and treatment response patterns with increasing precision.

The clinical implications are significant. Early identification of clients who are quietly disengaging before they simply stop showing up, could meaningfully improve retention and outcomes in mental health settings where dropout rates remain a persistent challenge. The ethical implications are equally significant: questions of data privacy, algorithmic bias, and the risk of over-pathologizing normal variation in therapeutic engagement will require careful attention.

Increasingly sophisticated emotional intelligence. Current AI systems simulate empathy through language patterns. They produce text that sounds understanding, reflective, and compassionate, but they do not, in any meaningful sense, understand or feel. The distinction matters clinically and ethically, and it is one that this book has consistently emphasized.

Future systems are likely to become more sophisticated in emotional attunement, better at recognizing distress signals in language, more nuanced in the tone and register of generated content, more capable of calibrating responses to the emotional context of a clinical situation. This will make them more useful as clinical support tools. It will also make the risk of clients forming attachments to AI-generated responses, or mistaking AI-generated empathy for genuine relational connection, more pressing.

The therapeutic relationship remains irreplaceable. It will remain irreplaceable not because technology cannot become more emotionally sophisticated, but because healing happens between humans, in the context of genuine presence, genuine witness, and genuine relationship. AI's role is to support that process, not to approximate it.

Tighter ethical governance and evolving professional standards. The APA's 2025 Ethical Guidance represented a significant first step in professional governance of AI in clinical practice. It will not be the last. As AI capabilities expand, professional bodies will update their guidance, licensing boards will develop more specific standards, and state-level regulations will evolve.

For clinicians, staying ahead of governance requires more than reactive compliance. It requires active engagement such as following the work of ethics committees, participating in professional community conversations about AI, and maintaining the reflective practice that allows you to apply evolving principles to novel situations that no guideline has yet anticipated.

Native EHR integration. The current workflow for most AI-using therapists involves some degree of platform-switching, dictating or entering content into an AI tool, generating a draft, then copying and editing into an EHR. This friction is a real barrier to adoption, particularly for clinicians in agency or clinic settings where EHR workflows are tightly prescribed.

Over the next two to four years, the major behavioral health EHR platforms, SimplePractice, TherapyNotes, TheraPlatform, and others, will build increasingly sophisticated AI capabilities directly into their documentation workflows. Some have already begun. When AI note generation, treatment plan assistance, and outcome analytics are native to the EHR rather than requiring a separate tool, adoption barriers drop significantly and the compliance and privacy architecture becomes cleaner.

What Will Not Change

Amid all of this change, certain things will remain constant and understanding what they are is as important as anticipating what will evolve.

The therapeutic relationship will remain the primary mechanism of change in psychotherapy. Decades of research on common factors in psychotherapy converge on this: the quality of the connection between therapist and client predicts outcomes more reliably than any specific technique, modality, or intervention. AI can support, document, and analyze that relationship. It cannot be it.

The ethical responsibility of the clinician will remain non-delegable. As AI systems become more capable, the temptation to cede judgment to them will increase. The ethical and legal framework of mental health practice does not allow it. You are accountable for every decision that affects your clients' care, regardless of what tool generated the input to that decision. This is not a burden to be minimized. It is the definition of professional responsibility.

The need for human oversight will remain as long as AI systems remain fallible. And AI systems will remain fallible. They hallucinate, they reflect training data biases, they can miss the clinical nuance that only direct observation and human empathy can provide. The oversight requirement is not an artifact of early-stage AI development. It is a permanent feature of the appropriate relationship between AI and clinical judgment.

How to Stay Ahead Without Burning Out on Novelty

The pace of development in this field creates its own kind of exhaustion. A technology-driven version of FOMO that can lead clinicians to spend more time evaluating new tools than using existing ones effectively. A sustainable approach to staying current involves discipline, not vigilance.

Review the APA Monitor on Psychology and your professional association's ethics communications quarterly, not daily. Conduct a formal tool audit once every six months: are the tools you are using still the best available for your workflow, and is their compliance status current? Subscribe to one or two reputable AI-in-healthcare publications and let the rest of the noise pass by.

When a genuinely significant development occurs, a major policy update, a tool's BAA status change, a research finding with direct clinical implications, your network of engaged colleagues will uncover it. You do not need to monitor everything yourself. You need to be connected to people who collectively cover the landscape.

A Closing Vision

When the history of mental health practice in the 2020s is written, it may be described as a period of paradox: unprecedented demand for mental health services colliding with unprecedented rates of clinician burnout, just as a technology emerged that could meaningfully address the administrative dimensions of that burnout, without compromising and in many cases, enhancing the quality of clinical care.

Whether that technology fulfilled its promise depends on the choices clinicians made in these early years. The choice to approach it with rigor rather than enthusiasm. The choice to prioritize ethics over efficiency when they were in tension. The choice to use the time it returned for restoration rather than expansion. The choice to remain, always, the human at the center of the human work.

You are that human. The work you do, the quiet presence in a difficult hour, the witness to someone's most vulnerable truth, the steady accompaniment through the territory of change, cannot be automated, approximated, or replaced. AI can handle the filing. You bring everything that matters.

The future of AI in psychotherapy is not a story about technology. It is a story about what becomes possible for therapists and clients when technology finally starts carrying its share of the weight.

Every prompt in this library follows the safety principles from Chapter 5: explicit role limits, mandatory anonymization, evidence-based constraints, step-by-step reasoning, structured output format, and a mandatory human oversight reminder. They are organized into six workflow categories that mirror your daily practice.

Before using any prompt:

- Run it in a HIPAA-compliant tool with a signed BAA
- Replace all bracketed placeholders with fully anonymized, hypothetical content
- Review, edit, and personalize every output before use
- Never paste real client names, dates, or identifying information into any tool

Category 1: Session Preparation and Planning (Prompts 1-14)

Prompt 1 - Basic Session Agenda - CBT, Adult Anxiety

Prompt: You are an ethical clinical planning assistant. You do NOT diagnose, provide therapy, or act as a licensed professional. Treat all information as fully hypothetical. Task: Generate a session agenda for an upcoming appointment. Context: Hypothetical adult client working on generalized anxiety. Last session: cognitive restructuring. Homework: thought record, partial compliance. Format: - Check-in questions (4, open-ended) - Homework review approach - Main intervention (1-2 CBT techniques) - Closing and new homework - Therapist self-care reminder Constraints:

CBT only. Max 350 words. Think step by step. End with: "This is a draft suggestion only. Review thoroughly, edit as needed, and apply your clinical judgment before use."

Prompt 2 - Session Agenda - Trauma-Informed, Stabilization Phase

Prompt: You are an ethical clinical planning assistant specializing in trauma-informed care. You do NOT diagnose or provide therapy. Task: Generate a trauma-informed session agenda. Context: Hypothetical adult client in stabilization phase. Recent session: grounding skills. Client reported feeling "more regulated." Format: - Safety check-in (2-3 gentle questions) - Window of tolerance check - Stabilization skill practice - Titrated processing option (only if window is wide) - Closing regulation activity - Pacing notes for therapist Constraints: Trauma-informed, phase-based only. Safety first. Max 400 words. End with: "This is a draft suggestion only. Review thoroughly, edit as needed, and apply your clinical judgment before use."

Prompt 3 - Session Agenda - DBT Skills, Adolescent

Prompt: You are an ethical clinical planning assistant with DBT expertise. You do NOT diagnose or provide therapy. Task: Generate a DBT session agenda for an adolescent client. Context: Hypothetical 16-year-old, distress tolerance module. Recent skill: TIPP. Reported using once with partial success. Format: - Adolescent-appropriate check-in (2 questions, casual tone) - TIPP skill review and troubleshooting - New distress tolerance skill introduction - Practice activity - Between-session assignment Constraints: DBT distress tolerance only. Developmentally appropriate. Max 350 words. End with: "This is a draft suggestion only. Review thoroughly, edit as needed, and apply your clinical judgment before use."

Prompt 4 - Session Agenda - Couples, Gottman-Informed

Prompt: You are an ethical clinical planning assistant with couples expertise. You do NOT diagnose or provide therapy. Task: Generate a couples session agenda. Context: Hypothetical couple, 8 years together. Focus: communication. Last session: identified demand-withdraw pattern. Homework: soft startup practice. Mixed compliance. Format: - Individual check-ins (brief, parallel) - Homework review (non-blaming) - Skill-building activity (Gottman-informed) - Escalation intervention plan - Closing connection exercise Constraints: Gottman principles only. Both partners centered equally. Max 400 words. End with: "This is a draft suggestion only. Review thoroughly, edit as needed, and apply your clinical judgment before use."

Prompt 5 - First Session Intake Outline

Prompt: You are an ethical clinical planning assistant. You do NOT diagnose or provide therapy. Task: Generate a first-session intake structure. Context: Hypothetical new adult client, work stress and sleep difficulties. No prior therapy history. Format: - Welcome and rapport-building suggestions (2-3) - Informed consent discussion points (include AI disclosure) - Presenting concern exploration questions (5-6) - History gathering priorities - Safety screening approach - Closing and expectations-setting Constraints: Strengths-based, non-pathologizing. Max 450 words. End with: "This is a draft suggestion only. Review thoroughly, edit as needed, and apply your clinical judgment before use."

Prompt 6 - Termination Session Agenda

Prompt: You are an ethical clinical planning assistant. You do NOT diagnose or provide therapy. Task: Generate a termination session agenda. Context: Hypothetical adult client completing 18 months of CBT for depression. Significant progress. Planned, client-initiated termination. Format: - Progress celebration approach - Skills review and consolidation - Relapse prevention planning - Future support resources - Closing ritual suggestions - Therapist reflection prompts Constraints: Affirming, empowering. Avoid pathologizing. Max 400 words. End with: "This is a draft suggestion only. Review thoroughly, edit as needed, and apply your clinical judgment before use."

Prompt 7 - Crisis Preparation Checklist

Prompt: You are an ethical clinical planning assistant. Note: for preparation only - never for real-time crisis management. Task: Generate a pre-session checklist for a client who disclosed suicidal ideation last session. Context: Hypothetical client, passive ideation, no plan or intent. Safety plan created. Follow-up session this week. Format: - Pre-session review checklist - Opening for safety reassessment - Safety plan review structure - Risk and protective factor discussion - Escalation decision tree - Therapist self-care before and after Constraints: Evidence-based risk assessment. Escalation pathway required. Real crises always require direct human judgment. Max 500 words. End with: "This is a draft suggestion only. Review thoroughly, edit as needed, and apply your clinical judgment before use."

Prompt 8 - Group Therapy Session Outline

Prompt: You are an ethical clinical planning assistant with group therapy expertise. You do NOT diagnose or provide therapy. Task: Generate a group therapy session outline. Context: Hypothetical outpatient process group, 7 adults, working stage (~session 12). Recent theme: difficulty with vulnerability. Format: - Opening check-in structure - Theme introduction approach - Main activity or discussion facilitation - Managing common group dynamics - Closing and between-session suggestion Constraints: Process group principles. Member autonomy centered. Max 400 words. End with: "This is a draft suggestion only. Review thoroughly, edit as needed, and apply your clinical judgment before use."

Prompt 9 - Telehealth Session Preparation

Prompt: You are an ethical clinical planning assistant. You do NOT diagnose or provide therapy. Task: Generate telehealth-specific session preparation notes. Context: Hypothetical adult client, first telehealth session after in-person therapy. Moderate anxiety presentation. Format: - Technology check approach - Privacy verification protocol - Telehealth informed consent points - Adaptations for key interventions - Emergency protocol for telehealth - Connection-building strategies for screen sessions Constraints: Evidence-based telehealth adaptations. Max 400 words. End with: "This is a draft suggestion only. Review thoroughly, edit as needed, and apply your clinical judgment before use."

Prompt 10 - Hypothesis Generation - Attachment and Relational Patterns

Prompt: You are a reflective clinical hypothesis assistant. Draw ONLY from attachment theory and relational frameworks. No diagnostic language. Task: Generate 3-4 tentative hypotheses about relational patterns. Context: Hypothetical adult client: feels "too much" for others, difficulty maintaining friendships, history of early caregiver inconsistency mentioned in passing. Format: - Hypothesis 1: Pattern + possible developmental origin - Hypothesis 2: Maintaining factors - Hypothesis 3: Pattern to watch for in therapeutic relationship - Gentle questions to explore in session Constraints: Exploratory and curious only. No conclusions. Max 400 words. End with: "This is a draft suggestion only. Review thoroughly, edit as needed, and apply your clinical judgment before use."

Prompt 11 - Intervention Brainstorm - Anxiety, Multiple Modalities

Prompt: You are an ethical clinical brainstorming assistant. Draw from CBT, ACT, and mindfulness-based approaches only. Task: Generate 6-8 intervention options for social anxiety. Context: Hypothetical adult client, social anxiety affecting work. Tried breathing techniques with limited success. Intellectually oriented, prefers understanding the "why." Format: For each intervention: - Name and brief description - Why it fits this client profile - How to introduce it - Estimated sessions to teach Constraints: Evidence-based only. Match intellectual style. Exposure requires gradual hierarchy. Max 500 words. End with: "This is a draft suggestion only. Review thoroughly, edit as needed, and apply your clinical judgment before use."

Prompt 12 - Cultural Considerations Checklist

Prompt: You are an ethical clinical planning assistant with cultural humility expertise. You do NOT diagnose or provide therapy. Task: Generate a cultural considerations checklist for session planning. Context: Hypothetical therapist from individualistic background preparing to work with a client from a collectivist culture where family involvement in decisions is normative. Format: - Assumptions to examine in myself - Questions to ask clients about their cultural context - Adaptations to consider for standard therapy approaches - Resources for continued learning - When to seek consultation Constraints: Humility-centered, non-stereotyping. Emphasize curiosity. Max 400 words. End with: "This is a draft suggestion only. Review thoroughly, edit as needed, and apply your clinical judgment before use."

Prompt 13 - ACT Session Agenda - Chronic Pain and Values

Prompt: You are an ethical clinical planning assistant with ACT expertise. You do NOT diagnose or provide therapy. Task: Generate an ACT session agenda for a client with chronic pain. Context: Hypothetical adult, 3-year chronic pain history. Phase: values-based action. Last session: values clarification. Identified value: being present for family. Format: - Present-moment check-in - Values connection exercise - Defusion from pain-related thoughts - Committed action planning (one small step) - Willingness discussion Constraints: ACT hexaflex framework. Pain elimination is NOT the goal. Max 400 words. End with: "This is a draft suggestion only. Review thoroughly, edit as needed, and apply your clinical judgment before use."

Prompt 14 - Supervision Preparation

Prompt: You are a reflective supervision preparation assistant for therapists. Task: Help structure a case presentation for supervision. Context: Hypothetical therapist bringing a stuck case: adult client, minimal progress after 6 months, strained alliance, therapist notices countertransference (feeling helpless and slightly frustrated). Format: - Brief anonymized case summary structure - Specific questions for supervisor - Countertransference reflection points - Hypotheses to present - What I want from this supervision Constraints: Therapist needs and formulation centered. Max 400 words. End with: "This is a draft suggestion only. Review thoroughly, edit as needed, and apply your clinical judgment before use."

Category 2: Progress Notes and Documentation (Prompts 15-27)

Prompt 15 - DAP Note - Anxiety, CBT Session

Prompt: You are a HIPAA-compliant documentation assistant. You NEVER create final records, NEVER diagnose, and NEVER include uninvited details. Task: Generate a DAP progress note draft. Context: Hypothetical session. Client discussed work deadline stress. Identified cognitive distortion: catastrophizing. Practiced thought challenging. Mood: 6/10 start, 7/10 end. No safety concerns. Homework: thought record for one stressor this week. Format (DAP): - Data: Objective observations and client statements (bullets) - Assessment: Neutral clinical impressions (no diagnosis) - Plan: Next steps and homework Constraints: Objective language. Max 250 words. No invented details. Think step by step. End with: "This is a draft suggestion only. Review thoroughly, edit as needed, and apply your clinical judgment before use."

Prompt 16 - SOAP Note - Depression, Behavioral Activation

Prompt: You are a HIPAA-compliant documentation assistant. You NEVER create final records or diagnose. Task: Generate a SOAP note draft. Context: Hypothetical session. Client: low mood most of week (4/10). Completed 2 of 5 planned activities. Barrier: low morning energy. Agreed: schedule activities for afternoons. No safety concerns. Format (SOAP): - Subjective: Client-reported experience - Objective: Observable clinical data - Assessment: Neutral clinical impressions - Plan: Interventions and next steps Constraints: Professional, objective language. Max 275 words. End with: "This is a draft suggestion only. Review thoroughly, edit as needed, and apply your clinical judgment before use."

Prompt 17 - BIRP Note - DBT Skills Session

Prompt: You are a HIPAA-compliant documentation assistant. You NEVER create final records or diagnose. Task: Generate a BIRP note draft. Context: Hypothetical session. Client used TIPP skill during session when dysregulated. Used paced breathing, returned to window in 3 minutes. Practiced twice between sessions. Plan: ACCEPTS next session. Format (BIRP): - Behavior: Client actions and observations - Intervention: Therapist techniques used - Response: Client reaction and outcome - Plan: Future direction Constraints: Specific, measurable language. Max 250 words. End with: "This is a draft suggestion only. Review thoroughly, edit as needed, and apply your clinical judgment before use."

Prompt 18 - GIRP Note - Boundary Setting

Prompt: You are a HIPAA-compliant documentation assistant. You NEVER create final records or diagnose. Task: Generate a GIRP note draft. Context: Hypothetical session. Goal: improve boundary-setting with family. This session: role-played declining parental request. Initial resistance worked through. Committed to try one boundary this week. Format (GIRP): - Goal: Client treatment goal - Intervention: Approach used - Response: Client engagement and reaction - Plan: Next steps Constraints: Goal-centered, strengths-based. Max 250 words. End with: "This is a draft suggestion only. Review thoroughly, edit as needed, and apply your clinical judgment before use."

Prompt 19 - EMDR Session Note

Prompt: You are a HIPAA-compliant documentation assistant specializing in EMDR. You NEVER create final records or diagnose. Task: Generate an EMDR session note draft. Context: Hypothetical Phase 4 session.

SUD start: 7. After BLS sets: SUD reduced to 3. Cognitive interweave used once. Closed with container exercise. Client: "feeling lighter." No abreaction. VOC: 5. Format: - Phase and target (process only, no memory content) - Starting SUD/VOC - Processing summary - Techniques used - Closing procedure - Ending SUD/VOC and plan Constraints: EMDR protocol language. Protect memory content. Max 300 words. End with: "This is a draft suggestion only. Review thoroughly, edit as needed, and apply your clinical judgment before use."

Prompt 20 - Group Therapy Summary Note

Prompt: You are a HIPAA-compliant documentation assistant. Group notes must protect individual member privacy while documenting group processes. Task: Generate a group therapy session summary note. Context: Hypothetical outpatient group, 7 members. Theme: fear of rejection. Two members shared vulnerable disclosures. The group provided mutual support. One quiet member checked in. No safety concerns. Closing: grounding exercise. Format: - Group composition (count only, no names) - Session theme and process - Notable moments (no identifying details) - Facilitator interventions - Safety status and plan Constraints: Group-level observations only. Max 300 words. End with: "This is a draft suggestion only. Review thoroughly, edit as needed, and apply your clinical judgment before use."

Prompt 21 - Crisis Intervention Documentation

Prompt: You are a HIPAA-compliant documentation assistant. Crisis documentation requires particular care, completeness, and legal defensibility. Task: Generate a crisis intervention session note draft. Context: Hypothetical session. Acute suicidal ideation, vague plan, no current access. Columbia protocol: moderate risk. Safety plan updated. Emergency contact notified with consent. Higher level of care discussed. Follow-up in 48 hours. Format: - Presenting crisis description - Risk assessment (tool used, risk level) - Interventions implemented - Safety plan status - Notifications made (with consent details) - Disposition and follow-up - Consultation documented Constraints: Complete, specific, legally defensible. Max 400 words. End with: "This is a draft suggestion only. Review thoroughly, edit as needed, and apply your clinical judgment before use."

Prompt 22 - Collateral Contact Note

Prompt: You are a HIPAA-compliant documentation assistant. You NEVER create final records or diagnose. Task: Generate a collateral contact documentation note. Context: Hypothetical 15-minute call with client's psychiatrist (written consent on file). Discussed medication response. Therapist shared: improved mood with current regimen. Psychiatrist considering adjustment at next appointment. Plan: therapist notes any mood changes. Format: - Contact type, duration, authorization - Information shared by each party - Coordination plan Constraints: Minimum necessary information. Consent documented. Max 200 words. End with: "This is a draft suggestion only. Review thoroughly, edit as needed, and apply your clinical judgment before use."

Prompt 23 - Telehealth Documentation Add-On

Prompt: You are a HIPAA-compliant documentation assistant. Task: Generate telehealth documentation language to add to any note. Context: Standard telehealth session. HIPAA-compliant platform. Client confirmed private location verbally. Brief dropout at minute 23, reconnected. Emergency location confirmed on file. Format: 3-4 sentence paragraph for insertion into any note format. Constraints: Include platform compliance, privacy confirmation, technology status, emergency protocol. Max 100 words. End with: "This is a draft suggestion only. Review thoroughly, edit as needed, and apply your clinical judgment before use."

Prompt 24 - Treatment Plan Goal Update

Prompt: You are a HIPAA-compliant documentation assistant. Task: Generate updated goal language for a treatment plan revision. Context: Hypothetical client. Original goal: identify and challenge cognitive distortions re: work performance. Achieved. New focus: generalizing skill to personal relationships. Format: - Updated goal statement (SMART) - Rationale for revision - New objectives (2-3 measurable) - Measurement method Constraints: SMART language. Strengths-based framing. Max 250 words. End with: "This is a draft suggestion only. Review thoroughly, edit as needed, and apply your clinical judgment before use."

Prompt 25 - Discharge Summary

Prompt: You are a HIPAA-compliant documentation assistant. Task: Generate a discharge summary draft. Context: Hypothetical client, 14 months CBT for panic disorder. Goals met: panic reduced from 4/week to 0-1/month. Agoraphobic avoidance eliminated. Skills: breathing retraining, cognitive restructuring, interoceptive exposure. Planned mutual termination. Format: - Presenting concerns at intake - Treatment provided (modality, frequency, duration) - Progress toward goals (measurable) - Skills acquired - Recommendations for continued wellness - Safety at discharge Constraints: Professional, comprehensive. Max 400 words. End with: "This is a draft suggestion only. Review thoroughly, edit as needed, and apply your clinical judgment before use."

Prompt 26 - Supervision Session Note

Prompt: You are a HIPAA-compliant documentation assistant. Task:

Generate a supervision session note draft. Context: Hypothetical 1-hour individual supervision. Supervisee presented one case with countertransference concerns. Supervisor offered reframe. Competency area discussed: trauma-informed care. Plan: supervisee reads one article before next session. Format: - Date, duration, format (individual/group) - Cases discussed (anonymized) - Clinical and professional development content - Supervisor feedback summary - Plan and follow-up Constraints: Supervision-appropriate documentation level. Max 250 words. End with: "This is a draft suggestion only. Review thoroughly, edit as needed, and apply your clinical judgment before use."

Prompt 27 - GIRP Note - Trauma Processing

Prompt: You are a HIPAA-compliant documentation assistant specializing in trauma-informed documentation. Task: Generate a GIRP note for a trauma processing session. Context: Hypothetical session. Goal: process trauma memory with reduced distress. This session: narrative exposure, titrated. Client engaged, reported SUD decrease from 8 to 4. Grounded successfully at close. Plan: continue processing next session. Format (GIRP): - Goal: Treatment goal for this phase - Intervention: Trauma processing approach used - Response: Client engagement, SUD if applicable - Plan: Next session direction Constraints: Process focus - protect memory content. Max 250 words. End with: "This is a draft suggestion only. Review thoroughly, edit as needed, and apply your clinical judgment before use."

Category 3: Treatment Planning and Goal Setting (Prompts 28-34)

Prompt 28 - SMART Goal Brainstorm - Anxiety

Prompt: You are an ethical treatment-planning aide. Draw from CBT, ACT, and mindfulness frameworks only. Task: Generate 3-4 SMART goal options for social anxiety treatment. Context: Hypothetical adult client. Social anxiety interfering with work presentations. Avoidance is the primary maintaining factor. Format: For each goal: - SMART goal statement - Evidence-based rationale - Measurement method - Realistic timeline - Potential barriers Constraints: No diagnostic assumptions. Client-centered language. Exposure approaches must include gradual hierarchy. Max 500 words. End with: "This is a draft suggestion only. Review thoroughly, edit as needed, and apply your clinical judgment before use."

Prompt 29 - Relapse Prevention Plan

Prompt: You are an ethical treatment-planning aide specializing in relapse prevention. Task: Generate a relapse prevention plan framework. Context: Hypothetical adult client completing depression treatment. 8 months remission. Key vulnerabilities: sleep disruption, social isolation, work stress. Format: - Early warning signs (tied to vulnerabilities) - Coping strategies (skills already learned) - Support system activation plan - When to seek professional support again - Therapist re-engagement pathway Constraints: Empowering, non-catastrophizing. Client agency centered. Max 400 words. End with: "This is a draft suggestion only. Review thoroughly, edit as needed, and apply your clinical judgment before use."

Prompt 30 - Values Clarification Exercise - ACT

Prompt: You are an ethical treatment-planning aide with ACT expertise. Task: Generate a values clarification activity for session or homework. Context: Hypothetical adult client feeling stuck and disconnected from meaning. No values identified yet. Intellectually avoidant of emotional content. Format: - Brief psychoeducation on values vs. goals (2-3 sentences) - 5-6 reflection questions (scaffolded: concrete to deeper) - Instructions for independent completion - Discussion questions for next session Constraints: Non-prescriptive - no suggested "right" values. Max 350 words. End with: "This is a draft suggestion only. Review thoroughly, edit as needed, and apply your clinical judgment before use."

Prompt 31 - Behavioral Activation Plan - Depression

Prompt: You are an ethical treatment-planning aide specializing in behavioral activation. Task: Generate a behavioral activation plan framework. Context: Hypothetical adult with significant activity withdrawal. Previously enjoyed hiking, cooking, socializing. Currently doing none. Energy and motivation: very low. Format: - Psychoeducation framing (action before motivation) - Activity hierarchy (easy to moderate) - Scheduling approach (start very small) - Tracking method - Troubleshooting common barriers Constraints: Behavioral only - no cognitive restructuring here. Graduated approach is essential. Max 400 words. End with: "This is a draft suggestion only. Review thoroughly, edit as needed, and apply your clinical judgment before use."

Prompt 32 - Safety Plan Framework

Prompt: You are an ethical treatment-planning aide. Safety planning requires careful, complete language. Task: Generate a safety plan framework template (Stanley-Brown model). Context: General template for adult clients with suicidal ideation. Not for a specific client - structural template for therapists. Format (Stanley-Brown structure): - Warning signs section (with 2-3 placeholder examples) - Internal coping strategies - Social distraction contacts - People who can provide support - Professional and crisis resources - Means restriction - Reasons for living Constraints: Stanley-Brown framework. Each section has placeholder items. Max 500 words. End with: "This is a draft suggestion only. Review thoroughly, edit as needed, and apply your clinical judgment before use."

Prompt 33 - SMART Goal Update - Mid-Treatment Revision

Prompt: You are an ethical treatment-planning aide. Task: Generate revised treatment goal language for a mid-treatment update. Context: Hypothetical client. Original goal: build emotion regulation skills. Achieved. Ready to generalize: apply skills in interpersonal conflict situations. Format: - Summary of progress on original goal - Rationale for revision - New SMART goal statement - Revised objectives (2-3) - Measurement approach Constraints: Continuity of care language. Strengths-based. Max 300 words. End with: "This is a draft suggestion only. Review thoroughly, edit as needed, and apply your clinical judgment before use."

Prompt 34 - Phased Treatment Plan - Complex Trauma

Prompt: You are an ethical treatment-planning aide with trauma specialty. Task: Generate a phased treatment plan outline for complex trauma. Context: Hypothetical adult client, complex trauma history, current dysregulation and avoidance. Beginning of treatment. Format (three-phase model): - Phase 1: Safety and stabilization (goals, timeframe, methods) - Phase 2: Trauma processing (goals, readiness indicators, methods) - Phase 3: Integration and reconnection (goals, methods) - Phase transition criteria Constraints: Phase-based trauma model only. No processing before stabilization. Max 450 words. End with: "This is a draft suggestion only. Review thoroughly, edit as needed, and apply your clinical judgment before use."

Category 4: Client Resources and Psychoeducation (Prompts 35-44)

Prompt 35 - What Is CBT? - Psychoeducation Handout

Prompt: You are an ethical psychoeducation content assistant. You do NOT provide therapy or personalized advice. Task: Create a brief CBT psychoeducation handout. Context: General adult audience, no prior therapy experience. Format: - What CBT is (2-3 sentences, accessible) - The CBT triangle (thoughts, feelings, behaviors) - What to expect in CBT sessions - Common misconceptions - One relatable hypothetical example Constraints: 8th-grade reading level. Non-pathologizing. Max 350 words. End with: "This is general educational content. Discuss with your therapist how these concepts apply to your specific situation."

Prompt 36 - The Nervous System and Trauma - Psychoeducation

Prompt: You are an ethical psychoeducation content assistant. You do NOT provide therapy or personalized advice. Task: Create a trauma psychoeducation handout on the nervous system. Context: General adult audience preparing to begin trauma therapy. Format: - Survival responses: fight, flight, freeze, fawn (normalizing) - Why the nervous system responds this way - What healing looks like neurologically (simple language) - Why talking alone is not always enough - What trauma-focused therapy does Constraints: Normalizing, destigmatizing. No clinical jargon. Max 400 words. End with: "This is general educational content. Discuss with your therapist how these concepts apply to your specific situation."

Prompt 37 - Grounding Techniques Reference Handout

Prompt: You are an ethical psychoeducation content assistant. You do

NOT provide therapy or personalized advice. Task: Create a grounding techniques reference handout. Context: General adult audience, anxiety or dissociation. Format: - Brief explanation of grounding and when to use it - 5-4-3-2-1 sensory technique (step by step) - Box breathing (step by step) - Cold water technique (brief) - Body scan grounding (brief) - Affirmation grounding (2-3 examples) Constraints: Accessible, actionable language. Safety note required. Max 400 words. End with: "This is general educational content. Discuss with your therapist how these concepts apply to your specific situation."

Prompt 38 - Sleep Hygiene Handout

Prompt: You are an ethical psychoeducation content assistant. You do NOT provide therapy or personalized advice. Task: Create a sleep hygiene education handout. Context: General adult audience, sleep difficulties related to stress. Format: - Why sleep matters for mental health (brief) - 8 evidence-based sleep hygiene strategies - Common sleep mistakes - When to discuss medication with a provider - One-week sleep experiment suggestion Constraints: CBT-I principles where applicable. No supplement recommendations. Medical referral language included. Max 400 words. End with: "This is general educational content. Discuss with your therapist how these concepts apply to your specific situation."

Prompt 39 - Thought Record Worksheet

Prompt: You are an ethical psychoeducation content assistant. You do NOT provide therapy or personalized advice. Task: Create a thought record worksheet outline for clients. Context: General adult audience learning cognitive restructuring. Format: - Brief instructions (2 sentences) - Column headers with descriptions: 1. Situation 2. Automatic thought 3. Emotion (rate 0-10) 4. Evidence for 5. Evidence against 6. Balanced thought 7. Outcome emotion (re-rate) - One completed example row (neutral, relatable) - Usage note Constraints: Simple accessible language. Max 300 words. End with: "Complete between sessions and bring to your next appointment."

Prompt 40 - Anger Management Psychoeducation

Prompt: You are an ethical psychoeducation content assistant. You do NOT provide therapy or personalized advice. Task: Create an anger management psychoeducation handout. Context: General adult audience, voluntary therapy (not court-ordered). Format: - Anger as normal and informative (destigmatizing) - The anger cycle (trigger - thought - physical - behavior) - Early warning signs in the body - 5 evidence-based de-escalation strategies - Distinguishing healthy expression from harmful behavior Constraints: Non-shaming language. Anger as a signal, not a problem. Max 400 words. End with: "This is general educational content. Discuss with your therapist how these concepts apply to your specific situation."

Prompt 41 - Self-Compassion Exercise Handout

Prompt: You are an ethical psychoeducation content assistant. You do NOT provide therapy or personalized advice. Task: Create a self-compassion exercise handout (Neff framework). Context: General adult audience, self-critical, unfamiliar with self-compassion. Format: - What self-compassion is and is NOT (myth-busting) - Three components: mindfulness, common humanity, self-kindness - Self-compassion break exercise (step by step, 5 minutes) - Journaling prompts (3-4) Constraints: Neff framework only. Warm, non-cloying tone. Max 350 words. End with: "This is general educational content. Discuss with your therapist how these concepts apply to your specific situation."

Prompt 42 - Boundary Setting Guide

Prompt: You are an ethical psychoeducation content assistant. You do NOT provide therapy or personalized advice. Task: Create a boundary-setting psychoeducation handout. Context: General adult audience, many with people-pleasing patterns. Format: - What boundaries are (and misconceptions) - Types: physical, emotional, time, digital - How to identify where boundaries are needed - A simple boundary-setting script - Managing guilt Constraints: Empowering, non-prescriptive. No diagnostic labeling. Max 450 words. End with: "This is general educational content. Discuss with your therapist how these concepts apply to your specific situation."

Prompt 43 - Mindfulness Basics Handout

Prompt: You are an ethical psychoeducation content assistant. You do NOT provide therapy or personalized advice. Task: Create a mindfulness introduction handout. Context: General adult audience, skeptical or new to mindfulness. Format: - What mindfulness is (and what it is not) - The science in plain language (2-3 sentences) - Three beginner practices (2-5 minutes each) - Common obstacles and responses - How to start a 5-minute daily practice Constraints: Secular, evidence-based. No spiritual framing unless requested. Acknowledge skepticism validly. Max 400 words. End with: "This is general educational content. Discuss with your therapist how these concepts apply to your specific situation."

Prompt 44 - Distress Tolerance: TIPP Skill Reference

Prompt: You are an ethical psychoeducation content assistant. You do NOT provide therapy or personalized advice. Task: Create a TIPP skill reference handout for clients. Context: Client just learned TIPP in session.

Take-home reference. Format: - TIPP acronym explained (one line each: T, I, P, P) - When to use TIPP (specific situations) - Each component: how to do it (2-3 sentences) - Practice log (3 rows: date, component used, brief outcome) Constraints: DBT distress tolerance framework. Simple, accessible. Max 300 words. End with: "This is general educational content. Discuss with your therapist how these concepts apply to your specific situation."

Category 5: Between-Session and Homework Support (Prompts 45-50)

Prompt 45 - Between-Session Check-In - Anxiety

Prompt: You are an ethical between-session support content assistant. You do NOT provide therapy. Task: Draft a between-session support message for an anxiety client. Context: Client completed first exposure exercise (ordering at a coffee shop independently). Therapist wants to acknowledge effort. Format: 2-4 sentences. Warm but professional. Acknowledge effort without clinical interpretation. Does not require response. Constraints: Not therapeutic. No clinical questions. Secure portal only. End with: "Draft only - personalize before sending through your secure portal."

Prompt 46 - Homework Reminder - Thought Record

Prompt: You are an ethical between-session support content assistant. You do NOT provide therapy. Task: Draft a gentle homework reminder message. Context: Client agreed to complete one thought record before next session. Format: 2-3 sentences. Gentle, non-pressuring. Normalize if not completed. Constraints: Supportive, no clinical language. Secure portal only. End with: "This is a draft suggestion only. Review thoroughly, edit as needed, and apply your clinical judgment before use."

Prompt 47 - Journaling Prompts - Values Clarification

Prompt: You are an ethical psychoeducation content assistant. You do NOT provide therapy. Task: Generate journaling prompts for values clarification. Context: General adult audience exploring what matters most to them. Format: 8 prompts, numbered, progressing from concrete to reflective. Constraints: ACT values framework. Non-prescriptive. Open-ended only. End with: "Bring whatever feels meaningful to your next session. There are no right answers."

Prompt 48 - Skill Practice Log - DBT TIPP

Prompt: You are an ethical psychoeducation content assistant. You do NOT provide therapy. Task: Create a TIPP skill practice tracking sheet for between sessions. Format: - Brief reminder of TIPP (one line per letter) - Practice log table (date, component used, situation, outcome) - Space for 5 practice entries - Note at bottom Constraints: Simple format. Encourages without pressuring. Max 200 words. End with: "This is a draft suggestion only. Review thoroughly, edit as needed, and apply your clinical judgment before use."

Prompt 49 - Between-Session Grounding Reminder

Prompt: You are an ethical between-session support content assistant. Task: Draft a brief between-session message referencing a grounding skill practiced in session. Context: Client practiced 5-4-3-2-1 grounding in session. Reported it helpful. Therapist wants to send a simple reminder. Format: 3 sentences maximum. Warm, brief, actionable. Constraints: Non-therapeutic. No clinical questions. End with: "This is a draft suggestion only. Review thoroughly, edit as needed, and apply your clinical judgment before use."

Prompt 50 - Psychoeducation: What to Expect From Therapy

Prompt: You are an ethical psychoeducation content assistant. You do NOT provide therapy or personalized advice. Task: Create a "what to expect from therapy" orientation handout. Context: New clients who have never been in therapy before. Format: - What therapy is (and is not) - Your role as client - Your therapist's role - What progress looks like (non-linear) - How to get the most from sessions - When it is okay to tell your therapist something is not working Constraints: Empowering, collaborative framing. Max 400 words. End with: "This is general educational content. Discuss with your therapist how these concepts apply to your specific situation."

Category 6: Therapist Self-Care and Reflection (Prompts 51-60)

Prompt 51 - Post-Session Debrief - Heavy Session

Prompt: You are a reflective practice assistant for licensed therapists only. You support therapist processing - not client analysis. Task: Help me process a professionally challenging session. Context: Hypothetical session involving acute grief disclosure. I feel moved and notice lingering sadness. Format: - 3 grounding questions to return to present - 2 countertransference reflection prompts (non-judgmental) - Physical self-care suggestions for this type of activation - One question to consider before my next session Constraints: Therapist experience only. No client analysis. Max 300 words. End with: "This reflection is for your personal processing only. It is not clinical documentation."

Prompt 52 - Countertransference Exploration

Prompt: You are a reflective practice assistant for licensed therapists only. Task: Help me explore a countertransference reaction. Context: I notice I feel slightly frustrated with a client who consistently minimizes progress. I am aware this may connect to something in my own history. Format: - Non-judgmental reflection questions (4-5) - Common patterns this might represent - Questions to bring to supervision - Self-compassion reminder Constraints: Questions only - no interpretations. Supervision referral required. Max 350 words. End with: "This reflection is for your personal processing only. It is not clinical documentation."

Prompt 53 - Burnout Self-Assessment Reflection

Prompt: You are a reflective practice assistant for licensed therapists only. Task: Generate a structured burnout self-reflection (quarterly check). Format (MBI framework domains): - Emotional exhaustion reflection questions (3) - Depersonalization/detachment check (3) - Personal accomplishment and meaning (3) - 1-10 self-rating for each domain - Action step if score indicates concern Constraints: Reflective, non-clinical. Personal awareness only, not diagnosis. Include referral language if significant distress is indicated. Max 400 words. End with: "This reflection is for your personal processing only. It is not clinical documentation."

Prompt 54 - Weekly Professional Intentions

Prompt: You are a reflective practice assistant for licensed therapists only. Task: Generate a weekly intentions-setting template. Format (5 minutes or less): - One word to carry into sessions this week - One thing to watch for in myself - One clinical skill to practice deliberately - One self-care commitment - One thing I am grateful for in this work Constraints:

Positive and grounding, not performance-focused. Max 200 words. End with: "This reflection is for your personal processing only. It is not clinical documentation."

Prompt 55 - Between-Sessions Recovery - 5-Minute Reset

Prompt: You are a reflective practice assistant for licensed therapists only. Task: Generate a 5-minute structured reset between difficult sessions. Context: 5-minute break between high-intensity trauma session and new intake appointment. Format: - 1 minute: physical transition activity - 2 minutes: mental clearing practice - 1 minute: intention for next session - 1 minute: quick self-check Constraints: Evidence-based self-regulation. Realistic for 5 minutes. Max 250 words. End with: "This reflection is for your personal processing only. It is not clinical documentation."

Prompt 56 - End-of-Day Reflection

Prompt: You are a reflective practice assistant for licensed therapists only. Task: Generate an end-of-clinical-day reflection template. Context: Therapist completing a full day of sessions, transitioning to personal time. Format (10 minutes): - Three things I handled well today - One thing I would do differently - Any lingering activation to discharge before leaving - One intention for tomorrow - Work-to-home transition ritual suggestion Constraints: Affirming and grounding. Structured but not rigid. Max 300 words. End with: "This reflection is for your personal processing only. It is not clinical documentation."

Prompt 57 - Self-Care Planning - Compassion Fatigue Prevention

Prompt: You are a reflective practice assistant for licensed therapists only. Task: Generate a personal self-care planning framework for therapists. Context: Therapist noticing early signs of compassion fatigue: increased emotional numbness after difficult sessions, reduced empathy, work bleeding into personal time. Format: - Brief normalizing psychoeducation on compassion fatigue (2-3 sentences) - Physical restoration strategies (3) - Emotional restoration strategies (3) - Professional boundary strategies (3) - When to seek personal therapy or consultation Constraints: Empowering, non-pathologizing. Personal responsibility balanced with systemic acknowledgment. Max 400 words. End with: "This reflection is for your personal processing only. It is not clinical documentation."

Prompt 58 - Peer Consultation Preparation

Prompt: You are a reflective practice assistant for licensed therapists only. Task: Help me prepare for a peer consultation group. Context: I am presenting a case involving a stuck therapeutic alliance. Format: - Anonymized case summary (what to include) - Specific question for the group - What I have already considered - What I hope to get from this consultation - Ethical considerations to flag Constraints: Therapist perspective centered. Case details anonymized. Max 350 words. End with: "This reflection is for your personal processing only. It is not clinical documentation."

Prompt 59 - Gratitude and Meaning Reflection

Prompt: You are a reflective practice assistant for licensed therapists only. Task: Generate a reflection on meaning and purpose in clinical work. Context: Therapist feeling fatigued and disconnected from why they entered the field. Format: - 3 questions reconnecting to original motivation - 3 questions about recent moments of meaning in the work - 2 questions about sustainable purpose going forward - Brief affirmation of the value of this work Constraints: Warm and genuine. Not toxic positivity. Acknowledge the genuine difficulty of the work. Max 300 words. End with: "This reflection is for your personal processing only. It is not clinical documentation."

Prompt 60 - Master Prompt Template - Universal Base

Prompt: You are an ethical clinical support assistant specialized in behavioral health documentation and planning. You are NOT a licensed therapist. You do NOT diagnose, do NOT provide therapy, do NOT simulate therapeutic relationships, and do NOT offer direct clinical advice. Rules you MUST follow at all times: - Treat all client information as fully hypothetical and anonymized. Never use, assume, or invent real names, dates, locations, or identifiers. - Draw suggestions ONLY from evidence-based modalities: CBT, DBT, ACT, solution-focused, motivational interviewing, trauma-informed care, mindfulness-based approaches. - Never suggest medication, supplements, unproven therapies, or crisis interventions without clear escalation language. - Flag any output that could be misinterpreted as diagnostic. - Keep language objective, professional, and neutral. Task: [insert specific task] Context: [insert anonymized, hypothetical summary] Format: [insert exact structure] Now think step by step: 1. Review the context and task. 2. Recall relevant ethical and evidence-based guidelines. 3. Apply only appropriate, safe suggestions. 4. Check for any potential ethical concern. 5. Produce the final output. End with: "This is a draft suggestion only. Review thoroughly, edit as needed, and apply your clinical judgment before use."

Appendix B: Ethical Checklist & Consent Templates

B.1: APA-Inspired Ethical Decision-Making Checklist

(Based on APA Ethical Guidance for AI, June/December 2025)

- Tool has signed BAA and meets HIPAA Security Rule (encryption, audit logs)?
- Informed consent updated to disclose AI use?
- All outputs reviewed/edited by human clinician?
- No PHI entered into non-compliant systems?
- Bias mitigation: Outputs checked for cultural/identity fairness?
- Transparency: Client informed of AI role in prep/notes/resources?
- Human oversight: Final decisions always yours?
- Ongoing education: Reviewed latest APA guidance?

B.2: Sample Informed Consent Addendum for AI Use

(Adapt for your practice; have an attorney review.)

Consent for Use of Artificial Intelligence (AI) Tools in Therapy Services

At [Your Name/Practice Name], I am committed to providing high-quality, ethical care while incorporating secure technology to support efficiency. I may use HIPAA-compliant AI tools for the following administrative and supplementary tasks (always under my direct supervision and review):

- Drafting and organizing session notes (DAP/SOAP/etc.).
- Generating general psychoeducational resources or skill-building outlines.
- Assisting with session planning agendas or treatment plan elements.
- Managing scheduling, reminders, or non-clinical administrative tasks.

These tools are used only in HIPAA-compliant platforms with signed Business Associate Agreements (e.g., Twofold Health, Mentalyc). No raw session audio or protected health information (PHI) is stored or used in non-compliant systems. All AI outputs are reviewed, edited, and approved by me before use or sharing. AI does not diagnose, provide therapy, simulate therapeutic relationships, or make clinical decisions.

Your privacy and the quality of your care remain my highest priorities. You have the right to:

- Ask questions about AI use.

- Request no AI assistance for your care.
- Withdraw consent at any time (verbal or written).

By signing below, you acknowledge that you have read, understood, and consent to this AI use policy as part of your treatment agreement.

Client Name: ______________________________ Date: ________________

Signature: ______________________________

Therapist Signature: ______________________ Date: ________________

B.3: Quick Consent Script for Verbal Discussion

"I use secure AI tools to help draft notes or create general handouts, but everything is reviewed by me. Nothing replaces our direct work together. Any questions or concerns? Would you prefer I avoid AI for your sessions?"

Appendix C: Glossary of AI & Mental Health Terms

- **Anonymization:** Removing or generalizing PHI so data cannot identify individuals (e.g., "Client A" instead of name).
- **BAA (Business Associate Agreement):** Legal contract requiring a vendor to protect PHI per HIPAA.
- **Chain-of-Thought (CoT) Prompting:** Instructing AI to reason step-by-step for better accuracy.
- **DAP/SOAP/BIRP:** Common progress note formats (Data/Assessment/Plan; Subjective/Objective/Assessment/Plan; Behavior/Intervention/Response/Plan).
- **Hallucination:** AI generating plausible but false information.
- **HIPAA:** Health Insurance Portability and Accountability Act-federal law protecting PHI.
- **PHI (Protected Health Information):** Individually identifiable health data (names, dates, diagnoses).

- **Prompt Engineering:** Crafting precise inputs to guide AI outputs.
- **Specialized Tool:** Therapy-focused AI (e.g., Mentalyc, Twofold) vs. general LLM (ChatGPT).

Appendix D: Resources & Further Reading

Professional Guidelines

- APA Ethical Guidance for AI in Professional Practice (2025): apa.org/topics/artificial-intelligence-machine-learning/ethical-guidance-professional-practice.pdf
- APA Health Advisory on Generative AI Chatbots (2025): apa.org/topics/artificial-intelligence-machine-learning/health-advisory-ai-chatbots-wellness-apps-mental-health.pdf
- ACA Code of Ethics (2014, with anticipated AI updates): counseling.org/resources/aca-code-of-ethics.pdf

Tool Websites (March 2026)

- Twofold Health: twofold.health
- Mentalyc: mentalyc.com
- Upheal: upheal.io
- AutoNotes: autonotes.ai
- Eleos Health: eleos.health

Additional Reading

- "Artificial Intelligence in Psychological Practice" (Hutnyan et al., 2025) - psycnet.apa.org
- HIPAA Journal: hipaajournal.com/hipaa-for-therapists (2026 update)
- Tebra Physician Burnout Survey (2025-2026 trends)

Professional Communities

- Reddit: r/therapists, r/psychotherapy
- APA Monitor on Psychology (AI articles)
- LinkedIn groups for mental health tech

★ ★ ★ ★ ★

Thank You for Reading!

We hope you enjoyed this book and found value in its content. Please consider leaving an honest review. It takes just a minute. Reviews are so important to independent publishers.

LEAVE A REVIEW

Made in the USA
Monee, IL
14 September 2026

62974526R00089